Also by Yiannis Gabriel

Freud and Society. London: Routledge

Working Lives in Catering. London: Routledge

Organizing and Organizations (with Stephen Fineman and David Sims). London: Sage

Organizations in Depth: The Psychoanalysis of Organizations. London: Sage

Experiencing Organizations (with Stephen Fineman). London: Sage

Storytelling in Organizations: Facts, Fictions, Fantasies. Oxford: Oxford University Press

Myths, Stories and Organizations: Premodern Narratives for Our Times. Oxford: Oxford University Press

Organizing Words: A Thesaurus for Social and Organizational Studies. Oxford: Oxford University Press

The Unmanageable Consumer (with Tim Lang). London: Sage

Return to Meaning: A Social Science That Has Something to Say (with Mats Alvesson and Roland Paulsen). Oxford: Oxford University Press

Music and Story

A Two-Part Invention

YIANNIS GABRIEL

authorHOUSE®

AuthorHouse™ UK
1663 Liberty Drive
Bloomington, IN 47403 USA
www.authorhouse.co.uk
Phone: UK TFN: 0800 0148641 (Toll Free inside the UK)
     UK Local: (02) 0369 56322 (+44 20 3695 6322 from outside the UK)

Published by AuthorHouse 02/17/2022

ISBN: 978-1-6655-9660-2 (sc)
ISBN: 978-1-6655-9661-9 (e)

Print information available on the last page.

Melody tells the will's secret story.
—Arthur Schopenhauer

Contents

Acknowledgements

This is a book for music lovers and a book for story lovers too. It sprang from my lifelong passions for melody (*melos*) and plot (*mythos*), the fruit of their marriage and their ability to excite and provoke each other.

The ideas in this book emerged over many years while listening to music in the concert hall or the opera house; on solitary walks; or while cooking, gardening, or lying awake in bed. They also emerged in conversations with many musical friends over decades, some of whom may recognize something in this book as theirs. I would like to thank them for being engaged interlocutors and fellow travellers on my musical journeys.

Above of all, however, I would like to acknowledge my deep gratitude to the composers whose music fills our lives with energy, meaning, and love. Without their inspired work over the decades and centuries, our lives would be so much poorer! Their contributions to our individual well-being and our collective cultural achievements are often overshadowed by those of great scientists, political, religious and other leaders. And yet, for many of us, Bach, Mozart, and Beethoven are no lesser benefactors of humanity than Prometheus himself.

My gratitude too to the many practicing musicians whose performances, live and on recordings, have kept the works of the great composers alive and who have opened for me a multitude of interpretations and insights. Some of them, as will become clear in the pages of this book, are my daily companions as I listen to their recordings for enjoyment, enlightenment, and inspiration.

Musical Discoveries

I am six years old, growing up on the fourth floor of an apartment block in the heart of Athens. I am having a quiet conversation with my father, when he asks me, 'Shall we listen to some music?'

'Yes,' I say to him, 'I like music.'

'You haven't listened to any music yet,' he retorts.

'*Of course*, I have,' I say. 'We hear music in church, in the car, on the radio, at school.'

'No,' my father persists. 'None of this is *real* music. Now, let's listen to some *real* music!'

He moves to a huge piece of furniture in our sitting room, which carries the badge Grundig. It is a musical factory of the 1950s and has several compartments. The top left part has a record player with 33, 45, and 78 rpm adjustments. In the middle, there is a radio with long-, medium-, and short-wave receptions. The right part contains a reel-to-reel tape recorder. The lower section contains a single huge speaker, as well as storage spaces for several records and tapes.

With great care, my father takes a heavy record out of the cabinet, removes the sleeve, and places it on the turntable. I hear a sound I have never heard before, the sound of a piano in Chopin's *Polonaise Héroïque*. It is one of those rare moments in life when our senses communicate something to us that is too beautiful, too shocking, or too incredible for our mind to take in. Later, I will have the same experience when tasting my first 'proper' curry in London's Kwality Restaurant or seeing a woman of such surpassing beauty that my mind refuses to believe what my eyes are seeing.

'*This* is real music.' My father's voice rises just above the sound of Witold Malcuzynski in the polonaise. 'It tells a story,' he continues, 'the story of a people, conquered and oppressed, who rise up against their oppressors. It tells the story of Polish patriots fighting to free their country from Russia. *Now,* you can *hear* the hooves of the cavalry galloping in the vast steppe pursuing the enemy … Now they pause for breath, dreaming of their proud country being free once again. They are inspired; they are determined to make whatever sacrifice it takes.'

My father's words have a mesmerizing effect on me. I can actually see the Polish cavalry. I can feel the feelings of the horsemen, their longing for freedom, their determination to make whatever sacrifice it takes to free their country from its oppressors. I ask to listen to the same music again. And again. Its effect is undiminished. I am totally enthralled. The world has changed forever for me. I have discovered what my father calls *real music*.

*   *   *   *   *

A short while later, my father invited me to listen to my second piece of real music, Smetana's *Vltava* or *O Moldavas* as it was then called in Greek. This was another inspired choice of music, one that again stirred his storytelling talents. It is a tone poem, a musical painting of Bohemia's great river as it springs from its twin sources, a cold and a hot one, growing in size and impetus, encountering along the way a forest hunt, a wedding of frolicking peasants, and a troop of water nymphs dancing in the moonlight before it reaches its majestic conclusion in a spectacular musical waterfall. All of this was narrated by my father as my imagination created a magical world that my senses could never deliver.

The impact of this music on me was again overwhelming. The sound of a full orchestra, the Cleveland under its legendary conductor Georg Szell, was unlike anything I'd ever heard before. As with the Chopin, I listened to *Vltava* countless times, coming to know every note by heart.

My musical education continued apace, first by listening endlessly to my father's couple dozen LPs and, slightly later, by attending the weekly concerts of the Athens State Orchestra at the Rex Theatre on Monday evenings. Beethoven's Fifth and the sound of Fate knocking on the door was my runaway favourite at the time. Seeing it performed in the concert hall by the Athens State Orchestra and its conductor, Andreas Paridis, left an indelible mark and probably gave me the idea to air conduct, flailing my arms around when listening to music on the turntable, a habit that took some years to shake off.

It took me a bit longer to encounter opera, my father never being a lover of the opera-singing voice. I don't believe I attended my first opera, *Rigoletto*, until I was nine or ten, an age at which I could understand the suffering of the jester but not the full ignominy of his daughter's predicament. I loved opera right away. And, when at age fourteen, I was given my first stereo, I started buying my own records, one of the earliest being *Rigoletto* sung by my beloved baritone Dietrich Fischer-Dieskau. Opera has remained one of the great passions of my life. In opera, music, drama, storytelling, and psychology achieve a very complex blend, communicating multiple and profound messages to its audience.

This book was inspired by my love for music, my firm belief that music can tell stories—sometimes explicitly, sometimes implicitly—and that these stories can help us make sense of some of our current troubles and challenges. When it succeeds, music offers narratives of sweeping emotional power but also of revelatory understanding. Music helps us understands ourselves and our fellow human beings. It helps us understand most elements and dramas that make up our lives, including politics, religion, leadership, sex, difference, love, and death.

Discovering a storyline in a piece of music is not always easy. Between what a composer intended to say, what he or she actually wrote down, what an interpreter expresses in performance, and what an audience understands tacitly or explicitly, there can be many discontinuities and gulfs. A musical composition may leave performers and audiences perplexed, especially on first hearing. This may be because it is abstruse or artless or because its takes time before its deeper meanings are uncovered. One can well imagine the sense of baffled incomprehension that greeted early performances of Beethoven's late string quartets before they were recognized as being among his profoundest utterances.

Performing traditions change too as historical sensitivities change. If each historical period discovers new meanings in Shakespeare's works, it is also true that it discovers new storylines in musical works. The period instrument movement that has revolutionized early music performances since the 1970s has enabled us to rethink classical works of the repertoire, listen to them with fresh ears, and discover new storylines that had laid dormant or undiscovered before. Similarly, operas have been rediscovered as producers and conductors update, reframe, or reset the action to highlight, for example, a feminist or an anti-colonial message in operas like Puccini's *Madama Butterfly* or Bellini's *Norma*.

Individual performers too can discover and reveal different storylines. In one of the chapters in this book I will show that a single piece of music, like Verdi's opera *Otello*, can tell different stories depending on how different singers interpret the score. Other pieces of music, ostensibly with no narrative programme, like a symphony or even a set of string quartets, can tell a story through their underlying musical structure and the musical language they deploy. My childhood's beloved Beethoven's Fifth Symphony is sometimes described as a journey from darkness to light, and even abstract music can attract sobriquets, like Dvorak's *New World Symphony*; Beethoven's *Moonlight Sonata*; and, indeed, Chopin's *Polonaise Héroïque*, that readily evoke a narrative or story.

This book was not written for specialist musical audiences. It is the work of a musical 'amateur,' a true lover of music—one who spends many hours every day listening to music, reflecting on it, and letting himself be moved by it. As a psychologist, I regularly observe myself listening to music and ask myself about the emotions it triggers, the connections it draws, and the problems it creates. Over the years, music has taught me as much about life in its infinite variety and complexity as many scholarly texts. I hope the musical stories that make up the bulk of this book excite and inspire other music lovers, maybe a little like my father's musical stories excited and inspired me, opening a lifetime of profound enjoyment, reflection, and learning.

Music and Stories

There is rarely a day in my life when I don't listen to music. Most days, I listen to music for at least six or seven hours. Music is a passion for me, as it is for countless others who concur with Friedrich Nietzsche's statement, 'Without music, life would be a mistake.' The success of radio programmes like *Desert Island Discs* or *Private Passions* indicates what a powerful presence music is in the lives of many of us—those who appear on these programmes and those who listen to them.

As an academic, I've been lucky to listen to music almost constantly when reading, preparing lectures, writing my academic books, or marking my students' assignments. I also listen to music when I drive, when I walk, when I cook, when I garden. Schubert, Beethoven, Bach, Mendelssohn, and many of the other classical composers are living presences in my life, occupying my thoughts and feelings more than anyone other than members of my family or my closest friends and colleagues. In my mind, they do not feature as Beethoven, Bach, and Mendelssohn but B (Beethoven), B1 (Bach), Felix (Mendelssohn), DSCH (Shostakovich), Nepo (Hummel), and so on.

I have listened to some of my favourite pieces of music hundreds of times and know them intimately. I believe it was the Hungarian violinist Joseph Szigeti who said that, having played the Beethoven Violin Concerto countless times, he knew it better than the composer himself. Beethoven composed it once and then moved on to other things, while Szigeti performed the piece again and again over his forty-year career. Could the same be said for us lovers of the concerto, who, with the benefit of recorded sound, have heard it many more times and in many more interpretations than the composer ever did or imagined?

Music and Story draws together my love of music and my other great passion, storytelling. As a Greek, I grew up in a culture full of stories, tales, and myths. As a child of the 1950s, I lived in a universe with no television, no screens, and precious few visual forms of learning or entertainment. Image in those days was firmly subordinate to story. Stories came out of the mouths of my parents and grandparents at the slightest opportunity; they came out of books and magazines, out of newspapers, and out of the radio. I listened to stories attentively and still remember vividly some of those I first heard before I got to primary school. Later in my life, I spent many years studying storytelling, collecting, analysing and interpreting stories, often returning to stories I had first heard as a child, as an army conscript, as an apprentice engineer on a merchant ship, and as a research psychologist in my field studies.

Drawing music and storytelling together came easy, once I had been initiated by my father's stories. Later, I came to see that much of the emotional power of music resides in the stories it tells, tacitly or explicitly. At its simplest, a religious hymn or a patriotic anthem communicate in tandem with the words. Music animates the words, making them memorable and amplifying their emotional power. A song or an aria can go further, expressing in a few minutes a great multitude of emotional states and nuances. Love, fear, anger, hope, envy, nostalgia, regret, disappointment, anticipation, the huge rainbow of human emotions can be represented through the power of music.

Music can express the conflict, turbulence and ambivalence of different emotional states, at times disclosing emotional truths about the characters words alone fail to communicate. It can reveal the subtexts beyond the literal meaning of the words being sung, the emotional depths beyond the lyrics. It can challenge or subvert the literal meaning of words. It can qualify or mock them. It can reveal the unconscious desires, motives, or vulnerabilities of different characters. Opera, as a large and complex musical genre, can highlight complex relations between different characters, with a huge range of emotions and nuances. When large groups of people sing together in choruses, music can disclose collective feelings of solidarity and community and invite the audience to share or oppose these feelings. In all these ways, sung music can tell stories of great variety and complexity.

Even abstract music, I will show in this book, draws its emotional power from the stories it tells. Some compositions make no secret of the stories that animate them. Tone poems and other forms of what is known as programme music are inspired by a story, an event, a natural phenomenon, or an abstract idea, offering a musical story that recreates or evokes the original. Tchaikovsky's *Romeo and Juliet Fantasy* and Sibelius's *Finlandia* are among countless examples of music that seeks to recreate and augment a narrative or an idea familiar to the listener. Other musical compositions can be more abstract, complex, or evasive about the stories they offer. As with works of literature, drama, or the fine arts, we often discover that, behind an overt story, lie many implicit or hidden stories. Sometimes, the story behind an abstract musical composition can be linked to the circumstances of its creation. Shostakovich's Fifth Symphony is a good example of a composition that will endlessly be debated and discussed. Is it 'a Soviet artist's creative response to justified criticism' as stated in a press article before its premiere, or does it express something darker and damning? Does the symphony end in a rousing conclusion in praise of the working class, or is the rejoicing forced, created by threat, as claimed Solomon Volkov in his book *Testimony*, ostensibly based on the composer's own words? Could the end be expressing no rejoicing at all but, rather, the stifled cry of a human being in deadly agony?

Beyond the circumstances of its creation, music can tell stories in purely musical terms. Relations between different musical ideas and tunes; harmonic conflicts and tensions; dynamic contrasts; rhythmical patterns; musical quotations and allusions; instrumentation; and, above all, the succession of moods and emotional tones can all fit into musical storylines every bit as recognizable and potent as those of oral and written narratives. Music can convey triumph; it can convey loss; it can convey love; it can convey betrayal; it can convey humour and satire; it can convey unbearable nostalgia and grief. It can convey these and much more.

This book is about the stories music tells and the beauty and emotional power of these stories. I will also try to show that musical stories, like other stories, are capable of reaching for deeper truths about ourselves, our relations, and our institutions. In line with Aristotle's theory of poetry, which studies what is general and timeless in contrast to history that studies the particular and the parochial, I will show that musical stories reach out for deeper truths about the human condition. When successful, they can provide dazzling insights into the lives we lead, with the joys and sufferings of life, its reversals, its errors, and its deceptions and self-deceptions.

But what exactly is a story? These days the idea of a story has been stretched to include virtually anything, including an image, a brand or a logo, a tweet, or a single word or a name. I prefer a more traditional idea of a story, as a text with a plot (what the Greeks called *mythos)* that has a beginning and middle and an end. A story is a text capable of generating strong emotion and that most precious resource, meaning. A story, both in its different parts and as a whole, creates and communicates meaning. The meaning of each part of a story depends not only on what has happened before but also where the storyline is going to conclude. 'Losing the plot' is an apt expression when a listener has lost the ability to figure out how events in a narrative are intertwined and, therefore, what their meaning is. In music too, different moments are interconnected, and their meaning is revealed through these interconnections. The meaning of a triumphant outburst of musical exuberance in a symphony alters if it is followed by a long dirge or lamentation. The meaning of the whole depends on the interconnections of the parts.

Another feature of stories highlighted by Aristotle is characters. Characters are individuals and groups with unique personalities, recognized in qualities such as kindness and cruelty, seriousness or levity, strength or weakness, independence or neediness. Characters can change in the course of a story; they can come into different relations with each other and can emerge and disappear in different ways. The same can be said about characters in music. Characters of musical stories can be identified with particular melodic ideas or rhythmical motifs; different instruments; different harmonies; or even single notes, each with its distinct personality. They can evolve and change in the course of a musical piece, entering into different relations with each other, including friendship, hostility, interdependence, or indifference. Powerful stories are those whose plots and characters invite strong feelings in the audience, such as compassion, fascination, love, and hostility.

Much the same can be said about musical stories. They are stories that open up new possibilities of understanding and even new possibilities of how we live our lives.

Like other stories, musical stories enrich our lives in many different ways. They entertain and stimulate in moments of boredom. They offer solace in times of despair. They create solidarity in times of loneliness. They liberate the imagination and open up visions of a better future. Musical stories can help us make sense of confusing situations and confusing emotions. There are even times when, as music critic Stephen Johnson observes in his book *How Shostakovich Changed My Mind*, music can bring us back from the edge of mental breakdown and spiritual collapse. Lastly, as I will show in the next chapter, music can become an important part of our personal story, of our very selfhood, something we value every bit as much as our most cherished experiences, something we seek to preserve and sustain because of the ways it preserves and sustains us.

First Acquaintances, Early Loves, Lifelong Companions

Listening to Tchaikovsky's First Piano Concerto earlier today brought to mind the frisson that I felt when I first heard this piece of music as a seven- or eight-year-old. The thrill of those opening bars in the horns, the piano's huge fusillades followed by the mighty octaves, and the puzzle and disappointment of the magnificent theme's quick disappearance never to be heard again is something I vividly remember.

I have very clear recollections of my first encounters with many different pieces of music. Mendelssohn's Violin Concerto, first heard at one of the Athens State Orchestra's weekly concerts, left me with a sense of disbelief—surely my ears were deceiving me; there just could not be sounds as beautiful as these. I had a similar reaction with Beethoven's Violin Concerto I first heard on a recording I borrowed from the school library. Ruggiero Ricci, the violinist on that recording, became one of my early musical heroes.

Such musical encounters were like love at first sight, unforgettable experiences that stay with us for the rest of our lives. Others take a lot longer to blossom. Beethoven's String Quartet Op. 130 was an early encounter. I heard it in a concert played by the Guarneri Quartet when about twelve, at the stunning Attalos

Stoa at the foot of the Acropolis, which was then briefly used for summer concerts. I found it totally incomprehensible. It took many listenings of the Amadeus Quartet recording before I felt that 'I got it.' It opened my ears to the depths of chamber music and became one of my lifelong intimate friends. I now understand why many of Beethoven's contemporaries, without the benefit of recordings, were totally perplexed by his late quartets.

Which then of these early loves endured and which faded away? Beethoven's heroic middle-period works had represented my supreme youthful ideals, highlights of a mythical universe of noble struggles, pitching the individual against the machine, art against the pedantry and grubbiness of politics, and the eternal against the parochial and provincial. Some of them fomented elaborate narratives in my mind. The *Pathétique* sonata, for instance, came to be associated with a long Russian narrative akin to Turgenev's *Fathers and Sons*. The Fifth Symphony was, for many years, my absolute musical summit, standing for the Promethean struggle of humanity against fate and misery. Most of these works lost their ability to move me by the time I reached my late teens. For several decades, I rarely listened to them. And then suddenly, about twenty years later, I started listening again to the *Eroica*, the *Emperor*, and their heroic siblings, not so much with a feeling of new discovery as with a sense of reunion with loved ones after a long separation.

Early in my musical explorations, I developed an infatuation for the sound of the violin, especially the virtuoso violin, epitomized by Paganini. Apart from its obvious athleticism, musical virtuosity stood for the quality of living life on edge, a devil-may-care attitude of living dangerously sharply at odds with the cosseted environment in which I spent my early years. It also embodied a willingness to take on impossible tasks and accomplish them in an almost effortless manner, through genius alone.

Schubert's *Rondo Brillant* for violin and piano D895, known for its virtuosity, is not one of his most famous or best pieces. Some have dismissed it as a pale derivative of Beethoven's *Kreutzer* Sonata. Yet, when I heard it on the Greek Third Programme, its virility and virtuosity truly thrilled me. Having heard it on the radio, I could not get it out of my mind. Yet, it was not possible to hear it again. Unlike today, when Spotify lists some thirty recordings of it, in the 1960s, it was unavailable in any of Athens record shops, and indeed there were hardly any recorded versions of it at all. Even when I visited London in 1967, I could not find it in the then mecca of Classical music, the HMV store on Oxford Street.

A single hearing had ignited a passion for this piece, almost like a person that we meet briefly and casually who then becomes an obsession for us. I re-encountered the *Rondo Brillant* sporadically whenever it was played on some radio programme or other but did not find a recording of it until the arrival of compact discs in the 1980s, when I finally bought a recording by Gidon Kremer. The CD is still in my collection, with the date of its acquisition 5 June 1992. Needless to say, by that time my passion for the piece had subsided, though it is one that continues to give me pleasure.

It is only recently that I realize that the Rondo's number in the Deutsch (D) catalogue places it next to the piano sonata D894, one of his least virtuosic compositions. They were both composed in 1826, two years before Schubert's death at the shocking age of thirty-one. The sonata, which I first heard played in recital by Vladimir Ashkenazy, has been one of my favourite pieces throughout my life. The same is true of virtually all of Schubert's mature masterpieces, most especially the sublime String Quintet, which I first heard on an old Saga recording played by the Aeolian String Quartet, while holding my breath as much for the beauty of the music as to exorcise those awful clicks and scratches, so common in the vinyl days. I have since had the pleasure of meeting and becoming close friends with Bruno Schrecker, now in his nineties, who memorably played the second cello part in that recording.

Wagner was one of my youthful idols. For a period, he totally eclipsed my love for Italian opera and even my adoration of Mozart's operas. I dread to think of the Siegfrieds and Parsifals I inflicted on my friends and relatives in my late teens and early twenties. Then, I let go of him. After many Tristans, Parsifals, and the odd Ring in the opera house and innumerable recordings, he became a stranger to me. Verdi, by contrast, returned to my affections where he has stayed ever since. During the years when Verdi's star was eclipsed in my mind by Wagner, I propounded various 'interesting' and foolish opinions of which I would be embarrassed now. By my early thirties, I had let go of Wagner altogether and returned to Verdi, young, middle-aged, and old man. I occasionally still listen to Wagner, but he is the one composer whose art I cannot dissociate from his political and other views, indeed his thoroughly unpleasant personality.

Over the decades of my life, I have discovered many new areas of music and, through them, new stories and new insights. Some of these discoveries were prompted by the enthusiasms of my friends. Hummel, for instance, is somebody who has given me immense pleasure in recent years and whose joyful compositions (with the exceptions of the glorious trumpet concerto and the wickedly mischievous mandolin concerto) had been entirely unknown to me. The film *Tous Les Matins du Monde* opened up the world of the viola da gamba repertoire, and more widely the French baroque, which has remained core to my listening affections and habits.

Mahler eventually installed himself in my musical heart and never shifted. Shostakovich arrived a little later. Like

Mahler, he has become a regular companion during my walks in the countryside. With others I have more erratic relations. For a long time, I jokingly said that I was saving Sibelius for my old age. I am now well familiar with much of his musical output, yet he has never become a true friend. Stravinsky and Bartok are composers who generally displease and vex me and who, with few exceptions, I tend to avoid. Bach, Mozart, Brahms, Schubert, Haydn, Dvorak, Tchaikovsky, Liszt, Chopin, Mendelssohn, and of course Beethoven are regular companions in my everyday life. Their music is rarely away from my ears, whether listening to it on speakers or headphones or in my mind's inner ear.

Overall, I recognize that my musical tastes are mainstream and conservative. Few pieces of contemporary music touch me or encourage repeated hearings. In the matter of interpretation, too, I would describe my tastes as relatively conservative, enjoying a beautiful sound and a traditional interpretation better than experimentation and novelty. I have not been swept up by the period instrument wave, although I recognize it has prompted us to listen to traditional repertoire with new ears. I generally remain loyal to many old-fashioned tried and tested interpretations, undoubtedly as they are imbued for me with a certain nostalgia. New approaches to the Beethoven Violin Concerto have questioned the orthodoxy of performing traditions going back to Menuhin, Kreisler and others who approached the piece with near-religious reverence and awe. Recent recordings by Patricia Kopatchinskaja, Isabelle Faust, and others make a strong case for a faster, freer, and more conversational approach, one I find stimulating and even enjoyable. Yet, I don't put away my old favourite versions by Grumiaux, Schneiderhahn, and Oistrakh. If anything, the new trends for bouncier and grittier sounds have made me return to Heifetz, Huberman, and Francescatti and listen to them with fresh ears and greater appreciation.

One tendency that has become widespread in recent years is for performers to make use of ugly sounds in pursuit of musical meaning. Instrumentalists as well as singers and even whole orchestras now will not shun harsh, strained, sour, and squeezed sonorities if, in their view, they help to communicate harsh, strained, sour, and squeezed emotions, like fear, anxiety, anger, and confusion. Even positive emotions like joy, exhilaration, hope, and love are frequently alluded to with sounds none too pleasing to the ear, as if to underline their fleeting or ambiguous qualities. I tend to admire and even applaud some of these tendencies, although my heart is unwilling to give up my love for sheer beauty of sound, the piano of Arrau or Rubinstein, the violin of Oistrakh or Grumiaux or the voice of Caballé or Bergonzi.

*   *   *   *   *

The chapters that follow are inspired by several pieces of music that are not only close to my heart but also capable of generating different insights into our lives, our politics, our anxieties, and our hopes. They are not necessarily those I love best, but they include most of those that have made me think longest. I hope that readers will be able to listen and enjoy these and other pieces with new insights, ending up by sharing my belief that music helps us discover new truths and new meanings about ourselves and our world, every bit as important as science, art, or literature. Beyond enjoyment and comfort, music provides shafts of enlightenment, something nobody has described as vividly as the teenage Nietzsche:

> God has given us music so that *above all* it can lead us upwards. Music unites all qualities: it can exalt us, divert us, cheer us up, or break

the hardest of hearts with the softest of its melancholy tones. But its principal task is to lead our thoughts to higher things, to elevate, even to make us tremble ... The musical art often speaks in sounds more penetrating than the words of poetry, and takes hold of the most hidden crevices of the heart ... Song elevates our being and leads us to the good and the true. If, however, music serves only as a diversion or as a kind of vain ostentation it is sinful and harmful. (Nietzsche in Young 2010, 37)

Reference

Young, J. (2010). *Friedrich Nietzsche: A Philosophical Biography*. Cambridge: Cambridge University Press.

Four Otellos, Four stories

Every song tells a story. Some composers, from John Dowland to Schubert, Schumann, and Mahler, were especially drawn to song, and poetry inspired some of their greatest compositions. Others, like Verdi and Wagner, made their home in the opera house, creating music dramas of great complexity and depth. Interpreters of songs, operas, and other musical genres involving the singing voice, like musicals, oratorios, and religious music, can tell the story in their own way, discovering different nuances and plot lines. Opera, in particular, has been the terrain of intense experimentation, since the pioneering production of Jonathan Miller's *Rigoletto*, which recast the drama from sixteenth-century Mantua to 1950s Little Italy, New York. Opera producers today routinely reinvent the storylines of the standard repertoire operas, inviting audiences to approach well-known works with fresh eyes, fresh ears, and maybe fresh hearts. In this way, they spark off vociferous controversies that keep opera in the limelight.

By its very nature, opera is a musical genre that invites many different interpretations. This chapter trims down operatic storytelling to the narrowest level; no production, no acting, just one particular role—Verdi's *Otello*, interpreted by four of its leading exponents.

Otello is one of my favourite operas, albeit one I've heard in the theatre less often than many others. It is an opera that makes great demands on the performer of the central character, taxing his vocal and interpretive qualities to extremes. It is not surprising that many famous tenors steered clear of this part altogether. Those who performed the role on stage and the recording studio are often remembered for their interpretation of this part above all other accomplishments.

The story is, of course, built on Shakespeare's immortal play. But Verdi and his librettist Arrigo Boito reconfigured it drastically, condensing many parts of the drama and introducing several scenes of their own. The opera, lasting just over two hours, packs the emotional impact of Shakespeare's original, and Verdi's powerful music underscores some of the central character's strengths and vulnerabilities and draws out very different musical qualities. As the triumphant leader of men in war, the part of Otello requires the full power of the dramatic tenor. Yet, in the magnificent love duet that concludes the first act, undoubtedly Verdi's greatest and a unique invention of his librettist, the singer must display great lyrical warmth. Then in the two acts that follow, he must portray the character's psychological and moral disintegration as Iago's poison seeps through. The final act requires the portrayal of a man so totally beside himself that he can commit cold-blooded murder followed quickly by a recognition of his folly and a convincing soliloquy before his suicide.

The four tenors I consider here, Mario del Monaco, Ramon Vinay, Jon Vickers, and Plácido Domingo, dominated the world stages over long periods of time, performing the part of Otello in different opera houses and leaving several recordings. They are each greatly admired for their interpretations, and their individual fans can rightly maintain that they were 'the greatest Otello of their era.'

Del Monaco has left us two 'official' recordings, partnered in both by the lovely but slightly overripe Renata Tebaldi and tormented by the not greatly rated Iago of Aldo Protti. Del Monaco's "Esultate," the hero's first entry after the defeat of the fleet of the infidel, is totally thrilling. This is a short outburst as the victorious Otello returns to Cyprus amid a raging storm and an anxious and near-riotous crowd. Del Monaco's voice pierces through the pandemonium created by the orchestra and the chorus—brilliant, secure, and perfectly in command.

And this maybe remains del Monaco's finest moment. He is the man you would want to lead your army into battle— heroic, self-possessed, and dominant. His vocal resources, the sheer loudness and virility of the voice, are matchless. Yet, as the domestic drama begins to engulf him, he quickly turns into the jealous husband, readily lapsing to hysteria. It takes the relatively artless Iago of Protti to derail him and send him into paroxysms of delirium far too quickly. One has no difficulty in thinking of him as the murderer of Desdemona; this is certainly an Otello who can kill. Yet neither murder nor suicide evoke the kind of pity on the part of this listener that the other three exponents of the part so amply generate.

Ramon Vinay sang Otello in a famous 1947 recording by Toscanini, partnered by Herva Nelli and Giuseppe Valdengo, fine artists both. He also sang the part several times for Wilhelm Furtwängler, leaving some off the air unauthorized recordings. The Toscanini was the first recording of Otello I bought as a first-year undergraduate in South Kensington and one that continues to move me deeply. I remember playing the final side of the LP set over and over again and thinking that tragedy in opera can never reach similar peaks.

Vinay's is a remarkable portrait of the part. Sounding a little more mature than del Monaco, he makes up in characterization what he lacks in brilliance. His tone is darker, and the voice seems to come from deep inside his being. Vinay brings out the true nobility of the character, a man undone not by his jealousy or his naivete but by his attachment to lofty ideals of comradeship, purity, and valour. I still find Vinay's fourth-act portrayal of the murder of Desdemona and his own final aria unsurpassed—going to the heart of the drama. Unlike del Monaco, this is not an Otello who can kill; he is a creature who has entered 'the dark night of the soul', a space where anything becomes possible. His final words are those of a true tragic hero, who belatedly comes to recognize the meaning of everything. Neither his crime nor his fall diminish him; if anything, they enhance his stature.

Plácido Domingo was the greatest living Otello for nearly thirty years or so, and his performances of the part are rightly celebrated. His three recordings of the opera are very consistent, in purely vocal terms, I prefer the second one he sang as part of the Zeffirelli film of the opera, even if, on his earlier recording, he received far better 'support' from Sherill Milnes as Iago, a great artist we once tended to take for granted, and the wonderful Renata Scotto.

Like Vinay, Domingo brings out the true nobility of the character so that his great monologue "Dio! My potevi scagliar tutti mali" ("God! You could have thrown every evil at me"), much of which he sang in Covent Garden while lying on his back, is almost unbearable. To see a great man reduced to this level makes almost as huge demands on the listener as it does on the performer. Domingo is also by far the most ardent and lyrical lover in the duet with Desdemona, and it is the voice that immediately comes to my mind when I think of the hero's unravelling in the great Act 3 ensemble when he virtually screams, 'But from myself I cannot fly!' ('Fuggirmi io sol non so ... sangue! L'abbietto pensiero!') Overall, I think that Domingo's Otello, like Callas's Tosca was a total operatic characterization—his suffering in the hands of the Iago of Sherill Milnes palpable, believable, and unbearable.

The fourth of our Otellos, Jon Vickers, was a singer I heard on stage several times, singing various Tristans and Sigmunds. On the one occasion, however, I was booked to see him in Otello I was struck by my usual operatic jinx. A no-show followed by a quick replacement by the then very popular James McCracken, who briefly surfaced in several recordings and whose Otello was in quite a different mould from the ones explored here.

Vickers's Otello is one that requires some getting used to. A huge voice in the theatre (in my experience 'bigger' in sheer volume than Domingo's), it was not one that recorded exceptionally well. His "Esultate" is less thrilling than our other three tenors, and his duet with the Desdemona (Leonie Rysanek in Vickers's first recording) takes some time to get going. There is something distant and aloof about this Otello that not even the expert baiting of Tito Gobbi, king among the Iagos, seems to penetrate. Vickers seems to inhabit a world of his own, an outsider, one carrying the seed of self-destruction deep inside him. Unlike Domingo and Vinay, who highlight the demise of the mighty hero, or del Monaco, who highlights the destructiveness of jealousy, Vickers seems to highlight Otello's isolation, the loneliness from which his marriage not only fails to protect him but actively exacerbates. This makes his utterance to Desdemona, 'You loved me for the dangers I had passed, and I loved you that you did pity them' ('e tu m'amavi per le mie sventure, ed io t'amavo per la tua pietà'), infinitely moving.

Having much admired Vickers in the central character's delirium in *Tristan und Isolde* or in *Peter Grimes*, I had expected him to overdramatize Otello's collapse in the Third Act. But he doesn't, at least in the recording with Serafin. Instead, his is a profoundly interior reading of the part, a man fighting his own demons, almost as if he inhabits a planet of his own. And this, of course, re-creates one of the essential qualities of Shakespeare's *Moor of Venice*. Vickers' Otello may not have the glamour of del Monaco, the power of Vinay, or the tragic nobility of Domingo, but it is the one I found most thought-provoking and, ultimately, the reason I compiled this brief survey. His is a total portrayal of the eternal 'other' and the sufferings and privations that ensue.

Four Otellos, fours stories. So when Otello sings 'Otello has his own supreme laws, love and jealousy, away with them!' ('Otello ha sue leggi supreme, amore e gelosia vadan dispersi insieme!'), just as the Cypriots arrive to serenade Desdemona, the words acquire a distinct meaning depending on which story you are following. The words of a jealous husband already intent on exacting his own justice? The words of a noble hero driven by duty? Or the words of a man apart from the others on a path to destruction? You choose!

The Three Graces: Beethoven's
Last Three Piano Sonatas

Opera, by its very nature, is a tapestry of narratives, some storylines visible, some not. Seeing the storylines of instrumental music is a little harder, although many composers and their publishers have helped listeners link specific compositions with different stories or images. Beethoven's 'named' piano sonatas, like the *Moonlight*, the *Tempest*, or *Les Adieux* readily evoke various moods that may prompt storylines in the listeners' minds. Chopin's *Heroic Polonaise*, as we saw earlier, spawned my father's gripping narrative about Polish patriots that permanently turned me into a music lover. Even abstract music with no thematic pretences can invite narrative and even mythological interpretations.

This is the case with Beethoven's last three of his thirty-two piano sonatas. These have always formed a unity, or even a trinity. Composed between 1820 and 1822, in the last years of the composer's life, they each have a special character but breathe the same air and speak the same language. They do not make for particularly comfortable listening and are less popular than the named sonatas, like the ones mentioned above. Yet, many music lovers view them as the apex of Beethoven's achievement in the piano sonata form, the culmination of what

German conductor Hans von Bülow referred to as the New Testament of the keyboard, Bach's '48' Preludes and Fugues of *The Well-Tempered Clavier* being the Old Testament.

While not the most popular with players or listeners, Piano Sonatas Nos. 30, 31, and 32 share a certain mystique sometimes associated with the word 'last.' Think of the Last Supper, last rites, and *The Last Tango in Paris*. Last is not only a signifier for a final will and testament; it also indicates a summation, a culmination, and a conclusion. It suggests closure but may also contain the seed of unrealized possibilities and potentials. 'Last' is often the tantalizing vision of what might have followed.

Beyond this mystique, Beethoven's last three piano sonatas share many musical and structural features—extensive use of trills, fugues, and variations; dense polyphonic and contrapuntal passages; but also some simple melodic lines that can be sung by the human voice, even a child's. Behind a flurry of notes, the listener who has spent time with the music can often discern some simple, even dance-like tunes.

And yet, many commentators have noted a quality that sets these sonatas apart from everything that has come before them. As with his last five string quartets, Beethoven's last piano sonatas seem to leave the world of 'normal' music behind them and visit spaces unseen and unheard by human beings before. The word 'spiritual' is often used to describe these spaces, although to me it does not begin to do justice to Beethoven's achievement. Some indeed see these three piano sonatas as some of the most advanced attainments of the human mind, at least in the sphere of music.

The fact that these sonatas often feature on a single CD (or 'album') makes them a trilogy, since many listeners absorb them in a single sitting, one of them starting as another fades out (although, as we shall see 'fades' only applies to the first and last of the three). A trilogy then or, better still, a triptych. Recently, however, I have come to see them more as three sisters than merely as a musical triptych, three characters of a single narrative with strong archetypal resonances. Thinking of them as three sisters brought to mind a short paper by Freud I have always enjoyed, first published in 1913, 'On the Theme of the Three Caskets.' The paper is inspired by the homonymous theme in Shakespeare's *Merchant of Venice*, in which three suitors of the fair and wise Portia are invited to choose one of three caskets, one made of gold, one of silver, and one of lead. The one choosing the casket that contains her portrait will win her hand.

The winner, Bassanio, is the one who chooses the least auspicious casket, the one made of lead. Through a sequence of interpretive pyrotechnics that take him to King Lear and his three daughters, the three Moerae (Fates) and the three Graces of Greek mythology, Freud argues that, behind the theme three caskets stands the archetype of three sisters, one of whom, the most special one, represents death. Through the unconscious defence of reaction formation, death becomes acceptable and even desirable by being endowed with special and most attractive qualities.

Stories involving three women are very common in folklore, mythology, literature, and music. Think of the three goddesses and the judgement of Paris. Think of Cinderella and her two ugly sisters or Chekhov's *Three Sisters*. The image of three sisters can be safely seen as a primal archetype in Western culture, a deep-seated and highly charged symbol that runs through humanity's unconscious and surfaces in dreams, literature. and art.

The three Graces of Greek mythology are a special case of this archetype and play a major part in Freud's interpretation. These three deities originally stood for three seasons of the year—spring, summer, and winter. Autumn did not enter the calendar as a season until later Graeco-Roman times. It is tempting to project springlike qualities to the first of these piano sonatas, the one in E, Op. 109. It opens delicately but determinedly with bell-like simplicity and maintains a spontaneous, joyful, and unexpected quality, as if different trees and flowers were blossoming in turn, with magical results. The concluding movement is a series of variations full of surprises on a simple hymnal tune, like nature coming alive in many wondrous forms. The sonata fades away with gentle repetition of the finale's opening theme. Spring will always return, no matter what.

The middle of the three sisters, the sonata in A flat, is certainly the most robust of the three, confidently melodic, generous, and warm. It can easily be seen as a summer sonata. It starts gently, almost where its predecessor ended, spring drifting into summer, but quickly builds into a songlike tune, which develops into a series of persistent upward moving figurations. Its momentum, warmth, and drive are reminiscent of the works of younger Beethoven, except for a very dark episode in the finale, an arioso of great pathos that could have come out of an operatic tragedy on Iphigenia. It is all swept away by a magnificent, resonant, and thoroughly confident fugue that I am sure Bach would have enjoyed, ending up in bounteous and sonorous triumph.

The last of the three sisters, the sonata in C minor Op. 111, is a different case. The C minor key was always Beethoven's turbulent and emotional key, the key of several stormy works, most notably the Fifth Symphony that starts with tragedy and ends in triumphant C major. It is hard to describe the extraordinary complexities of this movement designated *Maestoso—Allegro Con Brio Ed Appassionato* (majestic followed by fast, sonorous, and passionate). It starts with a peroration announcing a very confident and powerful motif that allows for a huge range of contrapuntal variations, some loud, some quiet, but all having the quality of inevitability that, to my ears, can sound almost machine-like. The powerful theme seems to swallow up all attempts by the second theme to introduce a more pensive or contemplative tone.

This second and final movement of this sonata is where Beethoven has saved his greatest surprise. It is a series of variations on a theme of the utmost simplicity and gentleness in C major. The variations become ever more ethereal, replete with trills and moving to the upper register of the piano without ever sounding harsh, instead becoming less and less earthbound. Devoid of anxiety and conflict, the music reaches ever greater heights of complexity and expression. Many commentators have noted their spiritual or other-worldly quality, as if Beethoven is leaving everything behind and is moving into new spheres of experience, devoid of tension, a state of musical nirvana.

The relation between nirvana and death was central to Freud's discussion of the death instinct in *Beyond the Pleasure Principle* (1920). Nirvana stands for the release from all terrestrial tension and strife, the aim of the cold and silent death instinct. This coldness, evocative of the dead body's frigidity, has long been a symbol of death, as captured admirably by Freud's most gifted disciple, C. G. Jung: 'We need the coldness of death to see clearly. Life wants to live and to die and to end. You are not forced to live eternally, but you can also die, since there is a will in you for both. Life and death must strike a balance in your existence' (2009, 274).

I long resisted the link between Beethoven's final piano sonata and the concepts of winter and death, but the more I reflect on it the more natural it seems. It is nothing to do with Beethoven having premonitions of his own death and all to do with the story the music tells and the ways it tells it, the trills, the ever-higher registers, nirvana awaiting at the end, the melting away of all tension and conflict. It is this Cordelia of piano sonatas that surely represents Beethoven's last will and testament in a genre in which he invented a new musical language of emotion, sensibility, and revelation.

An afterthought. The inquisitive reader may ask a plausible question. Have I fallen too easily for the seductive identification of Beethoven's last three piano sonatas with the Three Graces of antiquity? Wouldn't the same identification apply to other famous musical triptychs, like Tchaikovsky's last three symphonies bound together by the motif of ineluctable fate or providence? Or Mozart's last three symphonies? Or Schubert's last three piano sonatas, for that matter? Indeed, a case could be made for each of these triptychs, but it would stretch the patience of even the most indulgent reader. The spring-summer-winter analogy simply fails in every case. Take Tchaikovsky—granted, the Pathétique can be seen as winter, but can the Fourth Symphony be identified with spring? Scarcely? No, the narrative threads that tie these great triptychs together must be sought elsewhere.

References

Freud, S. (1913). 'The Theme of the Three Caskets.' In J. Strachey, ed. *Standard Edition, Vol. 12.* London: Hogarth Press, 291–301.

Jung, C. G. & Shamdasani, S. (2009). *The Red Book: Liber Novus*, 1st edn. New York: W.W. Norton & Co.

Gustav Mahler's Sixth Symphony: Images of the Apocalypse

In the course of a famous conversation on the nature of the symphony with Sibelius during a visit to Finland in 1907, Gustav Mahler said, 'The symphony must be like the world. It must embrace everything.' His Sixth Symphony, which had received its premiere the previous year, is undoubtedly a work that expresses this ambition—to embrace everything.

My relation to this symphony is quite peculiar and distinct from that to any other piece of music. Let me say immediately that it is the only Mahler symphony I have never heard performed live in a concert hall. It is also one of the very few pieces of music that still frightens me. Listening to it requires special attunements and maybe atonements too. The quiet moments before the final and cataclysmic hammer blow that brings the symphony to a close are ones I continue to find terrifying.

The symphony, occasionally referred to as *The Tragic*, is in four parts, involving a huge orchestra but no singers or choir. It can last anywhere between seventy and ninety minutes and makes immense demands on performers and listeners alike. It lends itself to many different interpretations of varying levels of introspection, tenderness, and brutality.

It also involves a number of puzzles, the main of which is the order in which the symphony's two central movements should be played. This is an issue Mahler did not resolve in his own mind. In the original composition and the symphony's first published edition, the enigmatic scherzo came before the elegiac andante. But in the symphony's premiere in Essen in 1906, Mahler reversed the order of the movements. Today, conductors and musicologists are divided on the order in which the movements should be performed, and attempts to establish Mahler's definitive view on this matter continue to be elusive. What is beyond all doubt is that the symphony offers a very different emotional and musical journey depending on the order in which these movements are performed.

My own preference is unambiguously for playing the scherzo before by the slow movement. In this way, the scherzo takes off where the massive first movement ends—it is almost a cruel parody of the first movement, at times seeming to disintegrate into farce (two drunks trying to find their feet out of a labyrinth) and, at others, evoking the innocence of children playing with no worries in the world. Placing the sublime andante third makes the start of the final movement truly shattering, especially if it follows with hardly any break. No final victory here, no relief and no consolation. Instead, a stark reality, which can be endured and understood but not triumphed over.

What makes this reality truly tragic is that whenever relief or consolation is in sight, it is tellingly crushed by what follows. Musical ideas that seem to carry the promise of something restorative or redemptive are subverted to reveal themselves as false promises. This is especially true in the finale, but it is also true within the symphony's overall architecture. If the andante is placed third, its noble and restrained beauty is shattered by the arrival of the finale, revealing itself as another painful illusion, eventually to be subverted and destroyed. Having the Scherzo after the andante somehow softens this blow. Playing the Scherzo after the opening movement offers another kind of subversion; the scherzo as a kind of ridiculing of the first movement's undoubted seriousness, twisting and undermining some of its serious musical ideas. I understand why other music lovers may see a different emotional architecture and logic in the piece. But for me, the case for playing the andante third is overwhelming—it is an issue of the emotional architecture of the piece.

Another issue that divides conductors is found in the hammer blows that punctuate the finale and lend it a terrifying power. Alma Mahler, the composer's wife and a not entirely reliable witness, quoted her husband as saying that each hammer blow represents a blow of fate as it strikes the hero, 'the third of which fells him like a tree.' Originally, the score specified five such blows, 'brief and mighty, but dull in resonance and with a non-metallic character (like the fall of an axe),' according to the composer, who later reduced them to three. In performance, Mahler omitted the last and maybe most important hammer blow, some say out of superstition. Conductors who, like Mahler, remove the final hammer blow have the option of softening the symphony's close, offering a more reflective conclusion—quite a contrast from the brutality of Mahler's original concept.

The symphony as a whole is sometimes viewed as portraying the journey of a tragic hero like Shakespeare's Macbeth through triumph, love, decadence, madness, and death. It certainly contains all of these elements, but this conception seems to me to diminish the music. By placing a single man at the centre (never a woman!), this interpretation blatantly ignores Mahler's ambition, which was 'to embrace the world'. Tragic heroes are but one element in Mahler's world; it also encompasses children's play and tender feelings, nature's beauties, the numerous absurdities of everyday life, and much else besides.

What makes this symphony quite unique, even among Mahler's works, is what I can only describe as its prophetic qualities. Written at the start of the twentieth century, as *La Belle Époque* was drifting into the nightmares of the trenches and the many nightmares that followed, Mahler's music offers a panorama of the century ahead in broad brushstrokes and tiny miniatures. Starting with armies on the march, Mahler encounters along the way lovers oblivious to the horrors that surround them, drunks, children and animals going about their business, science dreaming of technological Edens, machines of war, business, and pleasure—all ending in a final and total catastrophe.

This is a catastrophe that we the listeners are made to forget for long periods of the finale, which usually lasts more than half an hour and includes some of the happiest and most optimistic music Mahler composed. In several stretches during its unfolding, it seems to be leading to a major key heaven like so many other symphonies, not least Beethoven's Fifth. It is the shattering of all such hopes that makes this symphony such a devastating and unique emotional experience. It is also what makes the symphony prophetic, not only for the times when it was written but also for all times that precede a catastrophe.

Mahler's Sixth Symphony: One Story or Many?

A story can be told in many different ways. In each telling, the creative storyteller enriches it; embellishes it; and, at times, subverts it. So too can musical stories, when each performer discovers different possibilities and nuances. This is the art of interpretation, where the skill and imagination of the performing artist comes into its own. Mahler's Sixth Symphony has attracted a large number of interpretations on record, and this chapter explores the stories told in some of my favourite recordings.

The earliest recording in this survey dates from 1959. It is a live performance by my countryman Dimitri Mitropoulos conducting the Cologne Radio Symphony Orchestra a year before his untimely death. Mahler was infrequently performed in those days, and most orchestras were unfamiliar with his works. Mitropoulos, known for inviting orchestras to play their hearts out with no fear of mistakes, performs the symphony as a holy sacrament. Just as a priest in church scarcely notices a slip here or a fluff there, Mitropoulos is determined to give us the essence of the symphony, no matter what demands he makes of his orchestra.

The performance is full of mistakes and inaccuracies (especially from horns and trumpets)—but what a performance!

The opening of the symphony is heavy, heavy, heavy. Right from the opening march, feet dragging heavily on the ground, the sound is built from the bottom up, with drums especially prominent and persistent. One has a sense of a band of musicians being asked to play way beyond their capabilities, the conductor constantly demanding more expression; more weight; more dissonance; more commitment; and, towards the end, more despair. The rhythm is much more flexible than what we usually hear today, with microvariations even inside a single bar, which never sound contrived and which make the grotesqueries of the second movement especially effective.

Mitropoulos's slow movement is not without neurosis or trauma. This is a movement that evokes the adagietto of the Fifth Symphony and the first of the night musics of the Seventh, but Mahler holds a surprise up his sleeve. When we think that the movement is going to drift to a quiet end, like the adagietto, he produces a powerful climax that demands a crucial decision from conductors—is this climax a modest conclusion for the poetic beauties that have come before or should it presage the horrors of the final movement? Mitropoulos draws one of the most powerful climaxes from his orchestra, underlining the tragic qualities of the music, mixed with nostalgia for a lost world.

His finale is harrowing—an apocalyptic vision of horrors, punctuated by misleading episodes of hope and happiness that are swept away by the final denouement. In spite of the mediocre sound of the recording, the end leaves the listener drained. One wonders how it must have left the orchestra. The live audience remains as silent as they have been throughout the performance—no coughs, no throat clearing, no applause. This must have been truly a religious event.

Bernard Haitink's earlier recording with the Concertgebouw Orchestra is a different matter altogether. This is the recording by which I came to know the symphony in the early 1970s, and it is one well worth hearing today. For starters, it is wonderful to hear the symphony played by an orchestra that has always had supreme command of the Mahler idiom and plays the notes to perfection. In spite of this perfection, listening to it after Mitropoulos, I found the first two movements routine. The first movement (played here with the repeat of the opening theme, unlike in the Mitropoulos version) outstays its welcome, sounding repetitive and lost for ideas; the brass seem efficient but impersonal. It comes as a surprise then when, in the third movement, we enter a magical world, full of wonderful detail but with an overall architecture. This is noble music making that evokes the pastoral beauties of the earlier symphonies and almost comes to a quiet end before a climax that is thrilling in quite a different way from Mitropoulos—an apotheosis rather than a cataclysm. The finale is terrific—brazen brass, incredible woodwinds, and a memorable violin solo. But what happened to those hammer blows? They sound tame, like any ordinary drum, and not particularly loud either.

Leonard Bernstein's first recording (with the New York Philharmonic) is not one I've ever warmed to. It is generally too fast, too loud, and too melodramatic. The opening march is at the opposite extreme from Mitropoulos's—fast and furious, sweeping everything along its path. It is exciting, theatrical, neurotic, yes. But there is so much more that this music is trying to say, and it all gets lost here. The second theme of this movement is sometimes referred to as the Alma theme, after Alma Mahler's claim that it represented the composer's love for her. I have always found this claim implausible—the theme, far from romantic love, seems to inhabit the world of Mahler's *Kindertotenlieder* (*Songs for the Dead Children*), especially the unbearable second song in which the poet reminisces about his dead child.

Bernstein, in his earlier recording, misses the elegiac qualities of this theme, which, when played straight, becomes boring and repetitive (as does the bombastic theme that Mahler borrowed from Liszt's E-flat Piano Concerto). The second movement, played at exactly the same basic tempo as the opening one, starts effectively enough, with horns snarling. But again I ended up dissatisfied with the constant changes of tempo—the grotesque qualities Mitropoulos found in the missed steps here seem affected, evoking in my mind strange images of chickens missing their steps, maybe due to an overconsumption of alcohol.

Nor is the slow movement more to my liking. Constant and annoying changes in tempo, affected string slides, and an ineffective climax preceded by a huge ritardando all leave me unmoved. The finale, at under twenty-nine minutes the fastest in my survey, offers much drama and not a little melodrama— but no real fulfilment. The final climax is undoubtedly effective, but the preceding bars have failed to generate the sense of exhaustion and abject despair both Mitropoulos and Haitink achieve. There is plenty of anxiety in Bernstein's finale but little recognition (*anagnorisis*)—recognition of missed opportunities, of failed gods, of irretrievable loss— that gives this music its tragic grandeur. All of these qualities feature in trumps in Bernstein's later recording with the Vienna Philharmonic, a totally different matter from his earlier recording and one taking nearly ten minutes longer. It is also infinitely more powerful. The first movement retains its impetuosity but without brutality, the scherzo judged to perfection with lovely portamenti and apt hesitations but no affectations.

It is Bernstein's way of the third movement, however, that sweeps you off your feet. Played very slowly at over sixteen minutes, it transports you to the world of the Seventh

Symphony's night musics—tender, elegiac, and sad. If one did not know that Mahler would go on to compose a further three (four? five?) symphonies, this would truly be a valedictory movement, a farewell to the world, to life, and to love. The movement's climax has a haunting quality—not as powerful as some but with a sustained pathos that had me waiting for several minutes before I could brace myself for the terrors of the finale. This starts very nobly and gradually builds a dreamworld of nightmares and horrors, punctuated by two devastating hammer blows. Overall, this is a performance emotionally on par with Mitropoulos's but infinitely better played, except for the occasionally overly shrill sound of the piccolo, whose shrieking underlines the near-hysterical qualities of some of the music.

At the opposite extreme from Bernstein's second recording lies Abbado's 2004 recording with the Berlin Philharmonic, the winner of the Gramophone Record of the Year award in 2006. It was recorded live when the maestro returned to conduct 'his' orchestra following his recovery from serious illness. This recording is the first of Abbado's 'late' recordings, which now enjoy a most exalted status.

To my ears, this is a rationalist's interpretation, and a very sound one too. In spite of the occasion's emotion, Abbado keeps tight control of his forces, giving the impression of a conductor with a very clear idea of where he is going. The first movement is played to perfection—although it is slightly faster than Bernstein's, it lacks the latter's impetuosity and finds a wonderful range of colours with every return of the Alma theme.

I listened to the symphony as recorded, with the slow movement played second. This confirmed my view that, played this way, the slow movement comes too soon (we have not 'earned it' yet) and the scherzo too late, sounding almost redundant. Abbado's account of the andante moderato, at under fourteen minutes is the second fastest in my survey. It is beautifully played and sounds pastoral (especially the trio) rather than elegiac, the horn mellow rather than mournful. His climax brings a swelling of sound rather than the cataclysm brought about by Mitropoulos and (see below) Tennstedt.

The scherzo is played 'straight' with minimal tempo variations and, again, emphasizing the pastoral qualities, occasionally evoking the landler, which Mahler loved so much. The same is true generally of the finale, which is punctuated by two terrific hammer blows but overall holds back from excessive emotional display. Abbado's rationalist reading of the symphony is valid in its own right but creates much less electricity and pathos than do Bernstein's and others'.

I now come to a performance unlike any of the others I have listened to. Iván Fischer conducts his Budapest Festival Orchestra in what I will hesitatingly describe as a feminine rendering of this mighty symphony, toning down much of the shrillness and moderating the angst. Fischer builds the orchestral sound from the bottom, the cellos and basses and other strings providing a scaffolding so to say, which allows the trumpets to climb. The sound, throughout the symphony, is very homogeneous and beautiful. There is virtually no rasping or wailing brass, squealing or ear-piercing woodwind. Even the xylophone and the cowbells in this performance seem tame.

Fischer's andante is, like Abbado's, played second, and like Abbado's it is quite fast but breathes and sighs more expressively, to my ears frequently evoking a pastoral world of green fields and gentle nostalgia rather than overwhelming pathos. Even the hammer blows in the finale are 'civilized,' leaving the listener with a feeling that the symphony's 'tragic' soubriquet may refer to its bleak but not brutal ending, rather than its overall emotional tone. I was really fascinated by Fischer's ability to deliver such a plausible and satisfying account without plumbing the emotional excesses attempted by other conductors.

Emotional excesses describe to perfection my final version of the symphony in this survey, Claus Tennstedt's, conducting the London Philharmonic Orchestra. Even more than Bernstein's and Mitropoulos's, this is a performance that generates levels of terror, anxiety, and despair that one rarely experiences when listening to music. It is a performance that sums up for me what makes Mahler's Sixth so special.

From the start, Tennstedt takes his players and his listeners through an apocalyptic experience that, as I indicated earlier, sums up the symphony's core narrative. The opening theme of the first movement immediately evokes Nazi jackboots, and there is no romantic respite in the Alma theme, the conductor underlining instead its tragic similarities with the second song from the *Kindertotenlieder* cycle.

The scherzo is a brutal parody of what has gone on earlier, discovering no trace of the humour or the childlike innocence offered by other conductors. It is as bleak, morbid, and cruel as it can be, as if to underline that tragedy does not protect us from being ridiculous, something I also found in Mitropoulos's version. It is with the andante, however, that Tennstedt sets himself apart from all others. At 17:21, this is a full minute slower than even Bernstein's Vienna version and nearly three and a half minutes slower than Fischer's and Abbado's. At this pace, the movement can easily fall apart, and yet Tennstedt sustains its musical and emotional line and builds a climax like no other. This is no mere swelling of emotion; it is a true musical cataclysm that forces listeners to reach into the deepest recesses of their being to confront all the losses and all the regrets and disappointments that hide there. This is a musical experience not to be had casually or regularly.

Tennstedt's finale is, if anything, even more awe-inspiring. Although the timing suggests a slow performance, no other interpretation draws the listener nearer the precipice than this. Repeatedly, Tennstedt seems to almost lose control of the orchestra in a frenzied ride through every emotional landscape. Indeed, following the second hammer blow, the trumpets go completely off the rails, something I have come to treasure as a feature of this conductor's willingness to venture into forbidden and inaccessible territories.

At times terrifying, at others idyllic, Tennstedt's finale repeatedly offers glimpses of a happy end in sight, only to brutally shatter such allusions. Listening to it evoked in me thoughts of young Phaethon, the mythical character who rides the chariot of his father, the god Sun, through the skies, alternately inebriated and mortified, before crashing to his death. There is a moment when the music seems to drive towards a genuine triumphant conclusion, turning into a mad scramble, before collapsing into the quiet penultimate bars. The listener is, here, lured into believing the symphony will end in a whimper before the devastating final hammer blow brings the piece to its apocalyptic end. You will not have a more terrifying musical experience this side of Acheron.

Record Collecting

I remember vividly buying my first LP. It was a recording of Paganini's first two violin concertos played by Yehudi Menuhin, an LP with a bright red cover and a sketch of Paganini vividly engraved in my memory. I purchased the record from Discophil, the only shop in Athens circa 1966 that specialized in classical music. Dark, spacious, located in the city's fashionable Voukourestiou Street, Discophil was run by a distinguished-looking old man who I came to know well, as I became one of his most regular customers. I never saw any assistants in his shop. I never asked for his name.

Unlike today's easy and unlimited streaming, buying a record in those days was quite a process. Choosing a piece of music was usually guided by what I had heard on radio or at the Monday night concert of the Athens State Orchestra or, less often, by the recommendation of a friend or the fascination held by a name like *Jupiter*, *Fantastique*, or *Pathétique*. This last word was one that hugely excited my adolescent sensibilities. Entering Discophil was entering a cave of a myriad treasures, hundreds of LPs alphabetically placed by composer, names familiar and unfamiliar, each holding a promise of pleasures unknown. It also held the possibility of total incomprehension or even disappointment. What delights might Beethoven's *Archduke Trio* hold, Beethoven a name I already revered from

43

my acquaintance with the Fifth Symphony and the *Pathétique* piano sonata? And what enchantments might the sisters of my beloved's Chopin's *Polonaise Héroïque* hide? The oceanic immensity of classical music as a source of unlimited lifetime pleasures for the enthusiastic beginner is something I treasure and envy to this day. The inexhaustible possibilities for new discoveries in the record shop was in sharp contrast to the limited repertoire to be heard in Greece in those days in the concert hall or on the radio.

Bringing a new record home was, itself, a near religious experience. Opening the packet and admiring the LP sleeve, extracting the record with near shaking hands, and inspecting it closely before placing it on the turntable for the first time brought about an indescribable feeling of anticipation. The music released from the speakers of my primitive stereo system brought a near ecstatic feeling of pleasure and discovery. There were also times of deep disappointment, either because the music failed to fulfil its promise, as with the *Symphonie Fantastique*, or, more often, because the record had clicks and scratches that wrecked my musical enjoyment. I remember returning several records to Discophil and learning to inspect meticulously every new acquisition for scratches. It was then that I developed a particular respect for Deutsche Grammophon Gesellschaft or DGG as the 'yellow label' was referred to in those days. It was not so much that Karajan or Wilhelm Kempff or Dietrich Fischer-Dieskau or Wolfgang Schneiderhahn or any of the other great artists in its rosters was superior to those of other labels, as the quality of the pressings that always seemed immaculate and guaranteed a musical pleasure unspoilt by clicks and crackles.

Building a musical library in vinyl involved a great deal of care, learning, reading, and pondering. Records in the '60s cost 220 drachmas, approximately £3 or $7. Those were days of seemingly fixed prices before the inflation of the 1970s changed all that. At the time, 220 drachmas could buy you five or six meals in a quality Athens restaurant. Each acquisition was precious. Among my earliest records, I remember, of course, Verdi's *Rigoletto*, as well as *La Traviata* and *Trovatore*, the legendary set of Beethoven's symphonies with Otto Klemperer, Ashkenazy's doubling of Chopin's second piano concerto with Bach's first, Brahms's Third Piano Sonata, Beethoven's Third and Fourth string quartets, a disc of Schubert lieder based on ancient Greek themes sung by my hero Dietrich Fischer-Dieskau. Also, a recording of extracts from Wagner's *Tristan* in the classic Karl Bohm Bayreuth production, a recording that took a very large number of hearings before it started to release its love potion into my system; it was an intoxicating drug that took many years to work through, metabolize, and eventually cast off.

At the time, I also started receiving records from relatives, parents, and uncles returning from foreign trips, who I would ask to buy me exotic products unavailable at Discophil. Among them, I remember the records of Menuhin playing Bach Sonatas and Partitas for solo violin, as well as Paganini's 24 Caprices played by Ruggiero Ricci, an American violinist and early idol of mine. These were sourced by my uncle Alec at the HMV record shop on Oxford Street, a shop whose colourful descriptions by my uncle as the world's cathedral of classical music retail reduced poor Discophil to the standing of a provincial chapel. By 1968, I had paid my first visit to this cathedral, one I remember distinctly for the unbelievable privilege of being able to listen *and compare* LPs before purchasing in soundproofed individual booths. My first purchase, Dvorak's cello concerto played by Gregor Piatigorsky, followed a careful comparison with several others I sampled, and it drove home the revelation of how different the same music could sound in the hands of different performers.

After I arrived in London in 1970 to begin my studies in mechanical engineering, visits to the HMV cathedral became more regular, though even by the early 1970s, each record purchase required considerable research and reflection. By now I was a regular reader of *Gramophone*, which I had intermittently read earlier in Greece. I was also a fanatical listener of the Saturday morning *Record Review* programme on Radio 3. I still remember the first programme I ever heard in this series, a comparison of different interpretations of Brahms's autumnal clarinet quintet, and it was not long before I acquired the recommended version by Karl Leister and my beloved Amadeus Quartet.

In London, my live music experiences increased greatly too with regular visits to Covent Garden and the Royal Festival Hall. I was then able to hear in real life several of my musical heroes, many of whom remain indelibly in my memory—Rubinstein in Saint-Saëns's Second Piano Concerto, Fischer-Dieskau in Schumann songs, David Oistrakh in Tchaikovsky Violin Concerto, Carlo Bergonzi in *Ballo in Maschera*, Sviatoslav Richter in a recital that included Schubert's D958 piano sonata, Leontyne Price in *Trovatore*, Zino Francescatti in Walton's violin concerto, and many others. It was in the early 1970s that I also heard, for the first time, live, before acquiring any of their recordings, two stars who would dominate opera's world stages for decades to come—Plácido Domingo in *Tosca* and Luciano Pavarotti in *Rigoletto*.

By the time I went to Berkeley in 1974, I had built up a collection of some fifty odd records. Coming back from Berkeley in 1977, this had grown to well over three hundred, mainly thanks to the cheaper prices of classical records in the United States and the arrival of good quality 'budget recordings'. I bought my last LP in 1984. By this time my collection had grown to about 500. This was the year I bought my first CD, Ashkenazy playing Mozart's Piano Concertos 25 and 26. CDs were not cheap when they first arrived, retailing at £9 each, not much less than their current price. For the purpose of comparison, this was, at the time, the price of an amphitheatre ticket at Covent Garden. My CD collection grew slowly. I continued listening to music on LPs as well as cassette tapes well into the new century.

In the end, when moving houses in 2005, I found myself selling a handful of my LPs to a collector and donating the rest to Oxfam, not keeping a single one. Would I regret this? As it turned out, I have only ever missed one or two of my long-cherished LPs. In spite of the effort and care that had gone into their selection, purchasing, and constant transportation from house to house and record library to record library, it was the music I loved, not the physical object. Plus, with the arrival of CD, some of my most cherished LPs became available once again in digital form, something that has accelerated still further with the arrival of Spotify.

CDs brought the indescribable relief of not having to worry about scratches and surface noise. I built my collection methodically over the years, noting the date of each acquisition or gift and a serial number, a single number whether it was a single CD or a set of more than fifty, like John Eliot Gardiner's set of the complete Bach's church cantatas, which carries the serial number '1453', by coincidence, the year of the fall of Constantinople to the Ottomans. As I write these lines, I can see that my last CD has reached serial number '1559'. This is a delightful compilation of mandolin concertos on Vox, including those of Vivaldi and Hummel, that I hadn't heard since I had given away the vinyl version many years earlier. This turned out to be a reunion with an old friend, indeed an accidental reunion, as the CD was picked up by a friend in a second-hand store in the Netherlands without the friend knowing I had earlier had the vinyl version.

CDs brought another great boon. There was no need to turn over the record halfway. More importantly, the playing times of each CD increased as the buying public came to realize they paid the same price for an eighty-minute recording of Mahler's Second Symphony as they did for a forty-minute solo recital by an instrumentalist. As I am writing these lines, I am listening to J. S. Bach's *Magnificat* in the effervescent performance by John Eliot Gardiner and his forces, coupled with Emma Kirkby's radiant singing in Cantata BWV 51. It was bought for £9.85 in London on 29 May 1985 and carries the serial number '4.' It only has forty-one minutes of music on it, music that has given me immense pleasure over the years, but which represented rather short value at the time. Once record reviews started publishing the playing time of each CD, companies were forced to stretch the playing times to well above seventy minutes. This was a matter not only of better value for money but also of greater convenience, especially for people like me who listen to CDs while reading, writing, cooking, walking, or gardening.

How different the enjoyment of classical music has become today, with easy streaming of a bewildering variety of pieces and interpretations! Comparing Brahms's Clarinet Quintet on Radio 3's Building a Library in 1970 involved comparing the four or five versions available then. Today, Spotify lists no fewer than 100 different versions, available instantly at the click of a mouse. Where does the young enthusiast start? As with Google nudges, the tendency inevitably is to choose the top option on the menu or maybe the youthful-looking face on the cover or the hyped-up link that pops up on social media platforms. We become less selective and careful about our musical tastes. We taste; we sample; we like; and, more often than not, we let go.

The supply side of the classical music industry today has also changed beyond recognition. Many musicians are currently marketed as a 'product,' hyped up, managed, and raised sky high through exaggerated praise, only to disappear shortly afterward, eclipsed by younger, prettier faces. The lure of instant success and celebrity status is irresistible to many young musicians who rush to the recording studio in the hope of becoming celebrities through Spotify or YouTube. Nearly every young cellist these days will seek to record the Bach suites while still in their twenties. Works that were approached with a near religious reverence by earlier generations of cellists now become the playthings of performers seeking to find their 'voice' or make their mark. As it happens, I counted 365 versions of these suites on Spotify today, one for each day of the year! Hardly a month goes by without a new recording of Schubert's *Winterreise*, another work that used to inspire awe and call for artists in their full maturity. It is depressing to see how many honest, gifted, and even great performers are silenced in records and concert halls, simply because recording companies cannot find ways of 'packaging' them as the waves of fads and fashion come and go.

It is not all gloom, of course. One of the great advantages of streamed music has been the rediscovery of many recordings that had long been withdrawn and were unavailable to the buying public. A few days ago, I was wondering whether one may find any recordings by the Italian pianist Orazio Frugoni, now virtually forgotten, whose Vox record had introduced me to the magic of Beethoven's trinity of piano sonatas, *Moonlight*, *Pathétique*, and *Appassionata*. Imagine my surprise when I discovered the very recording on Spotify! My ears could once again experience sounds they hadn't heard for over sixty years. Admittedly, it is not an interpretation I would miss—the playing clean but a little wooden and the surface noise and abridgements, which include a substantial chunk of the finale of the *Appassionata*, presumably in order to fit the piece on the available space of the vinyl disc. Infinitely more musically satisfying and emotionally uplifting was to discover and watch a film of the great Rubinstein playing Saint-Saëns's Piano Concerto No 2 in 1975. This was the very piece I had heard him play with great poise, energy, and beauty a few years earlier in the Royal Festival Hall, an event that will remain forever in my memory.

Record collecting is no longer the art it once was. And maybe this doesn't matter. What matters is that every generation of music lovers, past and future, discovers the music afresh. Bach's sonatas and partitas for solo violin, Beethoven's Emperor Concerto, and Chopin's *Polonaise Héroïque* are being discovered every day, maybe even as you read these lines, by somebody somewhere—somebody experiencing their magic for the first time and beginning to make that magic part of their own life story.

Winterreise: Journeys into Darkness

The tradition of German song or lieder, sung by a single voice usually with piano accompaniment, takes some getting used to, especially for those of us not fluent in the German language. It is certainly not a tradition that appeals to the wider public. Nor are there any examples of lieder recordings attaining Top of the Pops status like Vivaldi's *Four Seasons*, Gorecki's Third Symphony, or Puccini's "Nessun Dorma". However, it amply repays the effort of listening to a singer and his or her accompanist with lyrics and translations in hand perform some of the most profound works in Western classical music.

While Beethoven and Mozart composed some wonderful songs, this is the genre dominated by the unfathomable genius of Franz Schubert, who died at thirty-one, leaving a legacy of over 600 songs. Many of them pack in four minutes as much drama as a four-hour opera. At the age of fifteen, Schubert had composed two of his greatest masterpieces—"Erlkonig" and "Gretchen am Spinraden".

Outstanding among Schubert's works is *Winterreise*, a cycle of twenty-four songs set to poems by the German poet Wilhelm Müller, composed in two remarkably short periods of time in 1827, the year before his death. The songs paint the journey of a young man who has been spurned by his lover as he wanders in bleak frozen landscapes, sinking into ever deeper despair and desolation.

Josef von Spaun, one of Schubert's friends, attended the first performance of the cycle's twelve first songs at a time when Schubert was not aware of the remaining poems. Von Spaun recalled the performance in a scene reminiscent of the Last Supper:

> For a time, Schubert's mood became gloomier and he seemed upset. When I asked him what the matter was, he merely said to me, 'Come to Schober's today. I will sing you a cycle of awe-inspiring songs.' He then, with a voice full of feeling, sang the entire *Winterreise* for us. We were quite dumbfounded by the gloomy mood of these songs, and Schober said that he had only liked one song, 'Der Lindenbaum.' Schubert replied: 'I like these songs more than all the others, and you will come to like them too.' (Cited in Bostridge 2015, x)

The cycle starts as the young man leaves behind the house of his beloved for the last time: 'A stranger I came, a stranger I leave.' There was talk of love, of marriage even, but he is now departing alone for a journey into cold darkness. In the first twelve songs, the young man casts his eyes back to moments of lost love and happiness, his beloved still a living presence, his feelings dominated by loss, anger, and bitterness.

In the second half, he sinks ever more deeply into solitude and despair, death coming to dominate his emotions and thoughts. His thoughts acquire a hallucinatory quality as a graveyard assumes the qualities of an inn, and he sees three strange suns rising in the horizon. In the final song, 'Der Leiermann,' he meets a hurdy-gurdy man, the first human he's encountered along his journey. 'Wonderful old fellow, shall I come with you? Will you grind your organ, for my tales of woe?' are his final words, in what some listeners see as a solitary glimmer of hope.

Müller's poems have a certain innocent sentimentality and a powerful visual imagery but were saved from oblivion by music of such consummate power, variety, beauty, and range that *Winterreise* remains unsurpassed in lieder and maybe in all song. It also represents the musical summation of German romanticism, in which the artist's feeling is the only law.

Winterreise makes the perfect walking companion—at seventy minutes, it keeps good company for a medium-size walk, which starts with "Gute Nacht" and finishes with "Der Leiermann". Several of the songs are propelled by an accompaniment that evokes the wanderer's footsteps, to which one can synchronize one's gait. Along the way, one enters Schubert's world, meeting occasionally the crows, the snarling dogs, the frozen river, the lime tree, the weathervane, the falling leaves, the three suns of the penultimate song.

I came to *Winterreise* in my late teens, buying my first recording during a trip in Switzerland. 'That will be the Fischer-Dieskau recording, sir?' asked the polite shop assistant, who was surprised to hear I had opted for the recording by Peter Pears and Benjamin Britten, a two-record set, which also included Robert Schumann's marvellous cycle *Dichterliebe*. I am not sure what the motive for that choice was, but I know that, once purchased, that recording was rarely away from my turntable. The sixth song, in particular, "Auf Dem Flusse"

("On the River") was one that evoked an emotion of desolation entirely beyond anything else I had heard until then.

Over the years, I have listened to many recordings of this cycle. While my musical preferences have changed, as have the fashions of interpreting the cycle, my love for this music has never wavered. I doubt there has been a month, including the summer months, when I did not listen to some recording of it or other.

Winterreise was originally composed for the tenor voice, but already in Schubert's short life, it was sung by lower male voices. More recently, there have been some outstanding interpretations by female artists, demonstrating that the songs not only tolerate transpositions into different keys but also draw special insights from different singers, young and old, male and female, native German speakers, and others. In the currently unfashionable but much cherished term, it is a 'timeless masterpiece'. What follows is a commentary of some of my favourite versions of this cycle. What I want to highlight is how different artists, through musical means alone, create different narrative lines and different emotions out of the same words, the same notes.

The first recording is by British tenor Ian Bostridge, accompanied by the fine Norwegian pianist Leif Ove Andsnes, first issued in 2004. The reason is that no other singer, in my view, comes as close to total identification with the cycle's central character as Bostridge, something maybe having to do with the fact that he is one of only two artists in this survey that I've heard perform the cycle live.

Bostridge's pure, crystalline voice captures the young hero's broken heart right from the start—such fresh voice, such deep pain. Alone, I think, among all interpreters, Bostridge communicates a kind of adolescent incomprehension of his predicament, a childlike naivete about the harshness of the world that arouses the listener's deepest compassion—what place is there for such an innocent in an indifferent hard world?

I find Bostridge best in songs that do not require a great deal of dramatizing. He captures to perfection the numbness of "Rast" ("Rest"), the inner misery of "Einsamkeit" ("Loneliness"), and the total isolation of "Der Wegweiser" ("The Signpost"). He uses most effectively a thinning and emptying of the voice—devoid of any vibrato, the voice turns white, like the landscape it depicts, sounding as if all emotion and energy has drained out of him. This happens, for instance, in the final verse of "Der Wegweiser", when he imagines the signpost pointing in the direction 'whence no man has yet returned'.

Bostridge is never found lacking in power and is exceptionally good at minute alterations in mood and emotion. A single word can insert a ray of hope in a bleak landscape or, conversely, ruin a comforting fantasy. In a tiny handful of songs, Bostridge sails close to the wind, with occasional mannerisms reminding the listener suddenly that this is, after all, a highly intelligent and sophisticated artist who has thought carefully every nuance of his interpretation. But this is a minor quibble when compared with the many insights he brings to the cycle.

In the final song, the sense of mystery and disbelief that has haunted Bostridge's journey from the start turn the hurdy-gurdy man into a figure of wonderment and veneration, the voice and the piano never rising above the merest whisper. It is a magical end to the journey, one that represents some kind of homecoming, although the listener is invited to figure out for themselves what kind of home this may be.

I turned from Bostridge to Peter Pears with some trepidation. Not only was his the recording that had acquainted me with *Winterreise*, but it is a recording that invited a cruel parody by Dudley Moore and was classed by the always entertaining Norman Lebrecht as one of the ten worst recordings of all time. I was also concerned that, since the '60s when Pears and his lifelong companion, Benjamin Britten, recorded the cycle fashions in lieder, singing had changed, favouring much more dramatic interpretations.

I needn't have worried. Pears and Britten's interpretation stands the test of time and gave me much food for thought. The voice is, of course, neither young nor fresh. Pears and Britten waited until they were nearly in their fifties before performing this Everest of the lieder repertoire. But I found energy, resonance, and, indeed, beauty in Pears's voice, even when I made direct comparisons with Bostridge.

Where Bostridge communicates youthful despair, Pears communicates bitterness, infinite sadness, and often nostalgia. The much-hackneyed view that this is an inner journey as much as an outer one undoubtedly seems accurate here. Listening to the unmatched tenderness Pears brings to "Der Wegweiser", and especially the touch of nostalgia in his interpretation, gave me the key—this is an older man reminiscing about his younger self, his lost love, his lost innocence. He does not need to dramatize images of death; he is close enough to it.

Some of the songs appear as if through a gauze in blurred colours—the snarling dogs are muffled, the crow is distant and even waking after the dream of love does not bring the desolation and despair it brings to other interpreters. Pears's unwillingness to overdramatize the songs, far from undermining their effect, accentuates their enduring power across space and time.

Pears's final encounter with the hurdy-gurdy man is moving beyond words, but in quite a different way from that of Bostridge. Instead of shaping every word to optimal effect, Pears gives the impression he has finally met his own double, his older self, through the eyes of his youthful alter ego. It almost makes me think that it is the Leiermann who has been telling his story all along, finally coming face to face with himself. There is no death or homecoming at the conclusion of this winter journey. There is no wonderment, but, rather, a stoic recognition of all the losses that add to make up a life.

The third singer in this survey is also a tenor, Peter Schreier, who I heard repeatedly live but sadly never in this cycle. He is accompanied by the great Sviatoslav Richter, whose legendary performances of Schubert piano sonatas made him a natural for *Winterreise* and give us a clue to the overall conception. Schreier and Richter set off at a funereal pace along their journey, reminiscent of Richter's opening of Schubert's last piano sonata in B-flat. This song, in which the young man is leaving the home of his lover for the last and final time, has a somnambulistic quality—so wrapped up in his thoughts is this traveller. He is carrying a big burden, and I can detect a touch of shame in the words: 'A shadow in the moonlight travels, along as my companion.' Has he stopped walking altogether as he contemplates the bleak future?

The second song, in which the weathervane evokes a bitter irony at his lover's fickleness, brings a total transformation in Schreier. There is sarcasm here, bordering on hysteria accentuated by the open-throated way he pronounces the vowel 'e'. The alternating qualities of total withdrawal and explosive vehemence become a trademark of this interpretation, highlighted by extreme tempos—very slow and very fast. With the help of Richter, Schreier creates a realistic portrait of a bipolar state of mind, of black depression and terrifying mania.

Schreier's wanderer is a dangerous man, something that could never be said of either Bostridge or Pears. He is one who, alone among all the interpreters in this survey, you may not wish to encounter along your way. This opens an interesting narrative possibility—could it be that his young lover became so scared by his mental instability that she decided a straight burgher would be a better prospect for the rest of her life? And who could blame her? Bourgeois life was never meant for Schreier, who reserves special venom for his rants against those asleep in their warm beds, dreaming their complacent dreams, while their dogs are barking after him ("Im Dorfe" ["In the Village"]). This is a superb realization and one that could be described not disparagingly as 'operatic' but not one for regular listening.

Three tenors—three great and very different interpretations, each taking its own view of this most extraordinary musical narrative. In the next chapter, we shall descend to see what happens when *Winterreise* is taken over by the baritone voice.

Reference

Bostridge, Ian (2015). *Schubert's Winter Journey: Anatomy of an Obsession*. London: Faber & Faber.

Winterreise: Further Journeys into Darkness

Tenor or baritone is a perennial question raised by *Winterreise*. Schubert composed the cycle for the tenor voice, which closely matches the youthfulness of its hero. It was also his own voice, in which he sang the cycle's first twelve songs to his bemused friends soon after their composition. Shortly before he died, he heard the cycle performed by his friend, the baritone Johann Michael Vogl, already in his fifties. The baritone voice makes up in expressive power and range what it lacks in freshness, and it is no accident that performances by baritones outnumber those by tenors.

Hans Hotter, the legendary Wotan of post-war years, sang the cycle many times and recorded it at least three. In 1954, he was partnered by the illustrious accompanist Gerald Moore in a version that has always been among my favourites. As Wotan, Hotter was famous for unleashing the might of the Valkyries with the merest vocal inflection. Such is the power and authority of the voice that he rarely raises it above a mezzo forte, and only in two brief moments of his *Winterreise* do we get its full Wagnerian force.

Aware that, with a voice like his, he could not possibly impersonate the cycle's young and fragile hero, Hotter opts instead to approach the cycle as a narrator, one who has lived with these songs for many years and knows their every nuance. He sings in long smooth phrases, in a voice remarkably even across the range, and the cycle assumes qualities of a sacrament. Narrator and listeners come together, knowing every detail of what lies ahead but determined to do justice to it and bring it to its conclusion in the proper manner.

In line with this approach, Hotter refuses to dramatize the text and lets his marvellous German diction communicate the words. The journey is a long one, and Hotter does not allow himself to relish occasional beauties or peculiarities here and there. Yet, as he moves to the hallucinatory and dangerous songs of the cycle's second half, he allows himself a tiny bit more urgency. The final song suits to perfection his deep baritone and is sung with total command. Hotter masterfully delivers his audience to their destination—the cathartic encounter with the hurdy-gurdy man whose song is addressed to one and all—*de te fabula narrator* (the tale is told about you). As the final note on the piano, played with the utmost delicacy by Moore, fades away, the listener experiences an overwhelming emotion of closure, almost tempted to say, 'Amen.'

I now turn to an outstanding baritone of the present generation, Matthias Goerne. Goerne's realization of *Winterreise* was part of the Hyperion complete edition of Schubert's songs, undertaken by the indefatigable pianist Graham Johnson, who accompanies Goerne on the piano.

Goerne sets off at a fair lick, dispatching the first song, "Gute Nacht", in just five minutes, the second fastest among those I sampled. More strangely perhaps, he does not vary his tone and adopts a somewhat casual attitude towards the cycle, which could not be more different from Hotter's reverential one. The next few songs seemed to confirm my impression of a slightly bland approach, a narrative one like

Hotter's but without Hotter's authority. I must confess that my concentration drifted away from the music once or twice.

How wrong I turned out to be. Somewhere near the end of the ninth number "Irrlicht" ("Will o' the Wisp"), I perceived a change; the voice becomes fuller, richer, the expression more varied. The words—'Every river finds its way to the ocean, / And every sorrow to its grave'—are sung with great sensitivity and total conviction. Thereafter, there was no doubt in my mind that this was an autobiographical, rather than a narrative account.

I came to view Goerne's approach in the earlier songs as one that maybe sought to create the impression of a man in the deepest shock of grief. Leaving the house of his beloved, he cannot bear to think or to feel—he is a person on autopilot. Gradually, as his wanderings take him away from the site of his trauma, he begins to reflect, experience, and feel; his delivery becomes more dramatic, the range of tones he draws on more diverse.

The cycle's eleventh number "Frühlingstraum" ("Dream of Spring") poses some of the greatest interpretive challenges to any performer. The first stanza offers a dream of happiness in green meadows, a dream cruelly interrupted by the crowing of the cock in the second stanza. The third stanza brings the dreamer back to the bleak reality of the winter—frozen leaves and desolation. The pattern is reprised in the next three stanzas, concluding with the fading hope of ever encountering love again. Goerne is utterly compelling here—I really don't think I have ever heard the third and the sixth stanzas of this song sung as beautifully before. In fact, the last three songs of the first part are sung with total conviction and extraordinary beauty.

I gradually came to see Goerne's interpretation of *Winterreise* as a journey into grief, starting with numbness, gradually drifting into regret, bitterness (though never too extreme), and acute depression but not despair. One constant in his interpretation is the beauty of tone unsurpassed by any of the interpreters we have considered thus far that never falters, even when the voice is tested to the limits, as in the closing verses of "Letzte Hoffnung" ("Last Hope"): 'I fall to earth as well / And weep on the grave of my hopes.' In some of the songs, like "Das Wirtshaus" ("The Inn") and "Die Nebensonnen" ("The false suns") this beauty is simply breathtaking.

As Goerne reaches the end of his journey, I was left with a total sense of emptiness and maybe depression. Not for Goerne the cathartic effect that Hotter creates by the end of the cycle—this journey ends in bleak darkness. This, contrasted with the singer's burnished vocal beauty (and maybe compounded by his powerful image on the cover of the CD), makes at least this listener want to grab him and say, 'Pull yourself together, big fellow. She was not worth it. There is more to life for you.' And this maybe is my one reservation about Goerne's deeply thoughtful interpretation.

Winterreise is very much a man's cycle. Yet, there have been some distinguished recordings by female interpreters, like Lotte Lehmann's from the early 1940s. In more recent years, there has been quite a spate of recordings from sopranos, altos and mezzos. I was personally quite reluctant to listen to the cycle sung by a woman until I heard it performed memorably some years ago at the Bath Music Festival by Brigitte Fassbaender. Fassbaender's interpretation removed any doubt in my mind about the ability of female singers to generate great insights and maybe find meanings in the cycle that elude their male counterparts.

In one of my recent walks, I reached the end of Goerne's *Winterreise* with some distance still to cover. I decided to listen to the last few songs in Brigitte Fassbaender's recording, starting with "Der Wegweiser", a song for which I have always had a special affection. It is another wanderer song, the bass line punctuating weary footsteps as the singer asks why he must always take the overgrown paths, hiding from other people even though he has done no wrong. He reflects how he is always heading away from cities and from life, before he concludes in the final stanza, 'Ahead I see a signpost / fixed before my gaze / I must follow a road / from which no man ever returns.'

Listening to Fassbaender in this song sent a shiver down my spine, something Goerne's version never threatened to do. The way she enunciates the last two lines is truly revelatory. Fassbaender inhabits a different domain from Goerne but also from every other interpreter we considered thus far (with the possible exception of Peter Schreier in some songs). Hers, like Hotter's, is a narrative approach, but it could not be more different from Hotter's. Where Hotter treats the whole cycle as a single entity, each song melting into the next, she dramatizes each song in a totally unique way, using her voice to shout, to speak, to caress, and occasionally to spit the text.

With the help of her accompanist, the composer Aribert Reimann, Fassbaender makes every word jump at you. Every step along the way is unique, frequently delayed, sometimes hesitant, occasionally missed. The rhythm changes are frequently even within a single bar as she tries to discover possibilities that are too risky or bring the voice to the end of the precipice. Sometimes she slides into notes or drags herself up to them—imitating the weary wanderer's unsure foot. Fassbaender's weathervane jerks wildly, her frozen tears bring cracks to the voice, the linden tree speaks like a ghost, the crow hovers, soars and swoops, the icy leaves sparkle.

Each song in Fassbaender's interpretation emerges as a complete drama or even a psychodrama. She tells the fate of her suffering hero but never comes close to sentimentality or even pity for him. Her job is to tell his story, not to shed tears for him—the tears are for the audience. What I find remarkable in this version is the explosive energy that Fassbaender generates. The songs never drift into each other. Every song marks a new beginning; in every song Fassbaender seems to find a new dimension, a new colour, and often a new voice. Following the turbulent end of "Der stürmische Morgen" ("Stormy Morning"), most singers sit back for "Täuschung" ("Illusion"), treating it as a reverie. Fassbaender, by contrast, tears into it, performing a wild dance with the words: 'A light does a friendly dance before me / I follow it here and there / I like to follow it and watch / The way it lures the wanderer.'

This is not a *Winterreise* for everyday listening. But then, who would want a version for everyday listening? Fassbaender makes big demands on her listeners. They must follow her closely with text in hand. They must be prepared to sacrifice beauty of tone for poetic effect. And they must be ready to be unsettled and disturbed. Above all, however, I feel that Fassbaender's mesmerizing reading forces her listeners to reach deep into their own souls, to discover all those winter journeys that lie buried there.

With Brigitte Fassbaender's dramatic account fresh in my ears, I turned to a younger interpreter, Christine Schäfer, whose version was chosen as the Building a Library recommendation by the BBC. Schäfer, who recorded the cycle with pianist Eric Schneider in 2003, has a light lyric soprano voice, something like the female equivalent of Ian Bostridge. Having heard her sing individual songs on the radio, I was interested to see how such a light female voice would cope with the demands of the cycle as a whole.

Schäfer's is undoubtedly a beautiful voice—pure, shimmering, and with a distinct virginal quality. Yet, it rarely 'sounds' beautiful in this recording. It frequently goes 'white' or spectral and even more frequently assumes a haunted, anxious quality. We only rarely get glimpses of its lyrical qualities in what is a highly dramatic interpretation, like Fassbaender's and Schreier's. However, lacking their dramatic vocal resources, Schäfer uses her extraordinary musical imagination to create quite a different type of drama.

Schäfer stamps her personality on the cycle right from the first song, the fastest rendering of "Gute Nacht" I have heard. She sets off in a sleepwalking manner, the notes falling like shards of ice on the frozen river. This is a truly suffering person, in a way that Fassbaender wasn't; she experiences despair and anguish but, above all, terror. What makes the reading unique is the haunted quality of her delivery, an instability that from the start suggests a person in a borderline psychotic state, a person who is pursued by visions and sees ghosts at every turn. In some songs, for example before the last stanza of "Greise Kopf" or after the first two verses of "Irrlicht", she seems to pause altogether, losing the line of her thought. This is no longer a narrative; at best, one could see it as free association. In other songs, the voice seems to imitate neurotic ticks and twitches. In yet others, it shrinks to the tiniest single thread, which threatens to break. The cycle's final word ('drehn' in her address to the Leiermann 'To my songs of owe / Will you drone your organ?') is sung like a siren's monotone, suddenly coming to a snuffed end, as if the life has finally been silenced. It is incredibly moving and effective.

As I listened to this interpretation, the image of Ophelia in 'virginal and vacant white' kept coming to my mind, a young woman crushed by a male world. Now, you may well ask, How does this square with the cycle's narrative, the jilted lover in his solitary journey through the winter landscape? Before trying to answer this question, let us consider two more qualities of Schäfer's delivery. Unlike Fassbaender or Hotter, who are very much performing the cycle to an audience, Schäfer is living the cycle like Schreier or Bostridge. However, unlike them and like Ophelia, she seems to be living it by retreating into a world of her own. What's more, this world, the listener often feels, is not much bigger than the room she finds herself in. The white head, the snarling dogs, the weathervane, the cemetery, and all the significant supercharged objects the traveller meets along his way but also the frozen river and the mountain crags all seem to be figments of her imagination.

Consider the crow, for instance. It is taken nearly at Schreier's ferocious speed. But instead of Schreier's weather-beaten face, here you see the face a fresh and beautiful girl—contorted by fear and anxiety, yes, but definitely not weather-beaten. Far from reducing the impact of her account, the sense that she is tormented by nightmares created by her own mind amplifies the tragedy of her predicament. This seems to be compounded by the exceptional beauty of the piano tone as captured in this recording. Her very alert accompanist seems determined to underline the intrinsic beauty of Schäfer's voice that we are only too rarely allowed to experience as she confronts her demons.

Let us return to the earlier question. How can Schäfer's feminist interpretation, a woman crushed by convention, square with the narrative's unalterable facts? This the story of a young man rejected in love, not the story of a young woman crushed by patriarchy. I was pondering this question for some time, when a memory of Schäfer surfaced in my mind, a memory of her at the very start of her career, singing *Lucia di Lammermoor* in an otherwise forgettable production with the Welsh National Opera, some thirty years ago. Theatre programmes are useful in such situations, since I was able to confirm that I had, indeed, attended this performance and that it was not a figment of my own imagining.

Now, Donizetti's *Lucia di Lammermoor* is miles away in every sense from *Winterreise*. But memories of Schäfer in her bloodstained white robe in Lucia's mad scene must have coloured what I was hearing here. Suddenly, it all seemed to fall into place. As I reached the penultimate song, the three suns in the sky, I realized I was hearing the voice of the girl who (like Lucia) had been forced to reject her poetic but unstable lover by her disapproving social milieu. He is dead now, and she is reading his poems, the surviving testament of his love, his solitude, and his despair. In my mind, I could not shake the image of Ian Bostridge as the poems' author.

Listening to the cycle again with this interpretation in mind, it all seemed to make perfect sense. Schäfer's account is pure theatre, pure psychodrama. And then an even stranger possibility arose. Could it be that, in her madness, she has reversed the roles of the rejector and the rejected? Could it be that she is the rejected one, abandoned in her solitary room by the excited poet, who could not settle down to bourgeois domesticity? She is now imagining the fate that awaits him. It is certainly a possibility, but then Schäfer's *Winterreise* is full of possibilities.

I shall not be returning to this *Winterreise* very often, and it surprised me that it was offered as the reference recommendation by distinguished musicologist Daniel Leech-Wilkinson on Radio 3's Record Review programme. Schäfer, however, demonstrates two things—first, what an exceptionally imaginative artist can do in performing *Winterreise* and, second, how *Winterreise* remains one of the greatest masterpieces of all Western music by speaking to those emotions that lie deep in every human soul, young and old, female and male.

Winterreise: The Journey's End

Dietrich Fischer-Dieskau's *Winterreise* has been my preferred interpretation for decades. His is the version to which I always turn when I want to listen to the music pure and simple, rather than to be challenged or tested. For me Fischer-Dieskau has always been the voice of Schubert. I left his reading of the cycle last because I wanted to see how it sounded after experiencing the great insights other interpreters bring to the music. I also wanted to compare two of Fischer-Dieskau's seven studio recordings from different parts of his recording career.

I start with what has long been my favourite recording, the 1971 version recorded with the great accompanist Gerald Moore as part of their monumental survey of nearly all Schubert songs for the male voice, originally on twenty-eight vinyl records and later on twenty-one CDs. In the first instance, it was the quality of Fischer-Dieskau's voice that raised his Schubert above everyone else's in lieder singing. His is a voice, like Callas's, that one can recognize among a million others. And just as Callas's voice was meant for Italian opera, Fischer-Dieskau's voice was meant for German lieder. The peerless legato; the perfect diction; the quick change of moods and timbres; and, above all, that natural lustrous sheen of the voice—the quality that created a halo when he sang Bach's *Matthew Passion*—all made the voice the perfect instrument for German romantic song. Add to these vocal qualities his extraordinary poetic sensibility and his outstanding musical intelligence and imagination, and you can see why his lieder interpretations remain reference points for subsequent singers.

In 1971, Fischer-Dieskau's voice was still youthful and beautiful, and his interpretation seems free of any hidden agendas. It is immediately apparent there is nothing pathological in this spurned lover, no bipolar condition as with Schreier or morbid depression as with Goerne. There is a full gamut of emotions here, but they're presented as 'healthy' emotions, if I can use this expression. Disappointment, loss, anger, nostalgia, hope, dejection, humiliation, defiance, and a degree of self-pity are all communicated as digested emotions rather than as 'raw' burning ones.

It is also immediately clear why Fischer-Dieskau is seen as having started a great lieder revolution by working closely with the text, probing the text, and even subordinating line and rhythm to the text. There is a tremendous amount of energy going into the poems and dramatizing too, as in Fassbaender's and Schäfer's powerful interpretations. But unlike these two, Fischer-Dieskau sees no ghosts and is not overwhelmed by creations of his own imaginings. He is a sensible and strong young man; he has been rejected by his lover and her family; he is devastated, but he is very definitely not deranged.

There is a great deal of pain here and sorrow too, but this is not a person unhinged by trauma. As a listener, I feel this man will eventually overcome his deep disappointment but will not forget it. This is a quest that will leave him less idealistic but 'wiser', a quest that marks the end of his youth. But even the angriest songs, like "Die Wetterfahne" ("The Weathervane"), which ends with the words 'their child is a rich wife,' does not leave him cynical.

Another thing. This is a reading for everyone, one that will move any music lover, irrespective of their age, their gender, or their musical tastes. While one is aware of a creative musical imagination here, this is not an interpretation that seeks to force new and unexpected meanings on the listener or come up with a different concept of the cycle as a whole.

Any grumbles? I am all too aware of the enduring criticisms of Fischer-Dieskau's tendency to accent particular words or force his tone into harshness in dramatic outbursts. Maybe my ears have adjusted by listening to singers like Schreier, Fassbaender, and Schäfer who are far more willing to venture into vocal ugliness in pursuit of musical meaning. The only song in which I found Fischer-Dieskau overdramatizing was "Mut!" ("Courage!"). This is a curious song, probably my least favourite in the whole cycle. Coming just before the two last transcendental songs, it represents one final attempt by the weary traveller to cheer himself up in a ninety-second manic outburst, 'When my heart cries out in my breast / I sing all bright and cheery.' Musically, this is a very important moment of lightness, splitting four very dark songs. But I felt that Fischer-Dieskau lapsed into rather too upfront jollity. The remaining two songs seemed ever so slightly diminished by this and did not reach the depths I encountered in other singers, especially Bostridge, Pears, Schreier, and Fassbaender. All the same, this is an interpretation for all seasons, one that has rightly stood the test of time and remains seminal.

For many years, I had avoided listening to any of Fischer-Dieskau's later recordings, aware of criticisms of the decline in his voice and, frankly, having persuaded myself that nothing could better the 1971 recording. When compiling this survey, I decided that the time was right to sample one of his later versions, choosing the 1979 recording with Daniel Barenboim, in preference to still later recordings with Alfred Brendel and Murray Perahia.

Coming at the end of my own long Schubertian journey, I must confess right away that this recording had me totally transfixed. It is not fundamentally different from the 1971 version, but nearly every direct comparison suggests to me greater depth, or what the Germans call *innigkeit*—poignant and intimate feeling. The opening song is infinitely sad, but tragedy has not set in yet. It ends gently, to be followed by a "Die Wetterfahne" ("The Weathervane") that suggests irony without sarcasm. "Wasserflut" ("Flood") is sorrowful, the song of a man who has tasted bitter disappointment but who is not at its mercy, a man who has lost much but is not defined by his loss. The words 'Da ist meiner Liebsten Haus', as in earlier recordings by this artist, marks a moment of deep recognition that makes this song a pivotal moment in the cycle.

My notes, as I listened to this interpretation, continue in the same vein. Every song seems to reach a new level of intensity and drama, but there is tenderness aplenty, as in the penultimate stanza of "Die Post". And notice too how perfectly all those z's of "Mein Herz" are enunciated. The whole of "Frühlingstraum"—but especially the last two verses as the voice sweetens and lingers as he tries to cling on to the thought of being reunited with his beloved—is consummate in its artistry.

Even this is surpassed by what I now think is the greatest account of "Der Leiermann" I have ever heard. In this last song of the cycle, Barenboim creates the bleakest frozen landscape with the simplest brushstrokes, against which the great baritone bares his soul. This is all barely audible and truly unbearable—a sorrow too deep for melodrama, a sorrow that engulfs the listener, leaving room for nothing else. Thank you, Schubert. Thank you, Dietrich!

Die schöne Müllerin: A Young Man's Simple Tragedy

Composed in 1823, five years before *Winterreise*, *Die schöne Müllerin* is the other great song cycle by Franz Schubert. Like *Winterreise*, it is based on poems by Wilhelm Müller; and like *Winterreise*, it describes the journey of a young man, a journeyman miller who falls in love with the miller's beautiful daughter, is rejected, and sinks into increasing despair, eventually drowning himself in the brook that has been flowing along, now peacefully, now restlessly throughout the cycle's twenty songs. The cycle closes with "Des Baches Wiegenlied" ("The Brook's Lullaby"), a gentle elegy to the dead youth.

Die schöne Müllerin is no *Winterreise*. The song cycle's central theme, the setting, and the central character have the simplicity of a folkloric universe—a universe of uncomplicated but powerful emotions, uncomplicated but gripping plots, and uncomplicated but thoroughly affecting characters. These qualities are reflected in Schubert's music—music that shares the miraculous lyrical qualities of the *Trout Quintet* and the Octet in F major, rather than the profundities of his last few piano sonatas and the string quintet.

What is the hero's name in Schubert's *Die schöne Müllerin*? This is not something the poet lets us in on. I suspect, however, that it is not Siegfried, Parsifal, or Agamemnon. More likely, he is called Hans, like the heroes in Grimm Brothers stories— the ordinary youth who falls in love, has dreams of future happiness, loses his loved one, and meets a watery grave in the stream that provides the backdrop for Schubert's composition.

In recent years, the cycle has been sung mostly by youthful tenor voices who can capture the protagonist's essential goodness and simplicity in ways that make his plight truly touching, if not tragic on the large scale. Outstanding among light tenor interpreters, in my view, have been Christoph Prégardien and Ian Bostridge.

What happens when a heroic voice attempts the cycle? Such, of course, is the voice of Jonas Kaufmann, a tenor who possesses a powerful and rich baritonal voice, currently singing a broad repertoire that includes many heavyweight roles (Parsifal, Sigmund, Don Carlo, and Otello). It is a voice that reminds me of Ramon Vinay, Helge Rosvaenge, and even, dare I say, of the great Caruso himself, in its vibrancy, depth, colour, and sheer power.

I have long admired Kaufmann's artistry on stage, where he must be counted as today's leading operatic tenor. I was excited, therefore, when a friend offered me his CD of *Die schöne Müllerin*, accompanied by the fine pianist Helmut Deutsch. Putting aside the CD's cover that allowed for a quiet chuckle, I wondered how a large, heroic voice would cope with the intimacies of this lyrical song cycle.

We know that big dramatic voices, like that of Hans Hotter, can find wondrous ways of interpreting Schubert, but I am not convinced that this was the case with Kaufmann. His interpretation is undoubtedly dramatic and even operatic. He looks for depths of expression that, in my view, are not in the text or in the music. His anger is oversize, his anxiety verges on the existential, and his grief is profound. But somehow the interpretation does not add up and leaves me constantly wanting less.

Kaufmann overinterprets the cycle, changing his colour and his tone several times in each stanza and being unwilling to let the songs communicate directly to the listener. He often scales his voice down, not by sweetening it but by hollowing it out, an effect much liked by German lieder singers today. But when applied to a heroic voice it makes it sounds husky and gruff; this would be suitable for Parsifal but not for the simple youth, in love equally with the heartless maiden and the stream itself.

When Kaufmann lets fly the big tenor, as in "Der Jaeger" ("The Huntsman"), the effect is undoubtedly powerful. But I can hardly imagine any lowlife huntsman standing up to this Siegfried of a man. I enjoyed best the last two songs, when, resigned to loss and to death, we hear Kaufmann's unaffected characterization, a worthy little requiem to the lost youth.

Listening repeatedly to Kaufmann's interpretation, I found my pleasure in the music itself gradually diminish, and I came to wonder if Schubert's level of inspiration here may not be quite what we have come to believe. I decided to turn to two other tenors who had given me pleasure in the past, neither of them heroic but not small voices either. Werner Güra's performance immediately restored my faith in the music's lyrical perfection as the ideal complement to the poems' folkloric qualities—the voice natural with no dynamic extremes, the emotion tenderly portrayed to match the states of an ordinary young man in trouble.

Even better, I thought, was Peter Schreier, a tenor who I have long admired but one who can be irritating at times in his vocal mannerisms. Not having listened to his cycle for more than five years, I was suddenly gripped by notions of hearing a Mime type of character (the devious dwarf in Wagner's

Siegfried, a role that Schreier had sung with great effect) pursuing the fair maiden of the mill. I needn't have worried. Schreier, accompanied by the peerless Andras Schiff, gives us an interpretation to treasure—lyrical, sensitive, responsive. He tells the story of the hapless youth and his simple but deeply moving predicament to perfection, while the brook flows quietly in the background. For the time being, his will remain my preferred tenor interpretation for this treasured score. As for baritones, I am sure the reader already knows my tastes in this matter!

Mahler's Little-Known Symphony No 0

Many music lovers know of Bruckner's Symphony No 0, *Die Nullte*, the symphony its composer dismissed as worthless juvenilia. But did you know of Mahler's Symphony No 0? It is undoubtedly the work of a young man, but nobody would dismiss it as juvenilia.

It is a large-scale symphony in E major lasting nearly an hour. If you listen to it knowing nothing about it, you will be forgiven to think that it is somewhat 'derivative'. You can hear a great deal of Wagner here, some Brahms and Dvorak too, and even some Elgarian 'nobilmente' from time to time. Above all, you will recognize Mahler in each of its four movements, in nearly every theme, every march, every counterpoint, and every chorale. You soon realize that describing it as derivative is hollow. The music has power, it has sweep, it has imagination. It is, for lack of a better word, the work of genius. So why have you and most music lovers never heard it? Why is it so rarely performed in the concert hall? And why does the mighty Amazon only list a small handful of recordings of it?

Well, to start with, it is not by Mahler at all. It is the work of Hans Rott, an Austrian composer born in 1858 who briefly shared accommodation with Mahler. Ah, this figures! He must have been influenced by the great man, I can hear you say, until we learn that Mahler's First Symphony appeared some ten years *after* Rott's Symphony in E. Completed in 1880, Rott's symphony also prefigures Bruckner's mighty Seventh Symphony, the only other great symphony in E major, by three years.

Rott's story is a sad one. A highly promising student, he excelled in his organ studies with Bruckner and showed remarkable talent in composition. His family circumstances were tragic; he lost both parents by the time he was eighteen and faced grave financial difficulties. Worse, his early compositions, including the opening movement of what became his Symphony in E major, received hostile response from the musical establishment, including Brahms himself. Shortly after the completion of the symphony in 1880, while travelling on a train to assume a minor post as choirmaster in Mulhouse, Rott suffered a major psychotic episode; he imagined Brahms had filled the train with dynamite and threatened a fellow-passenger with a firearm. He was then confined to a mental institution, where he died a few years later, having destroyed many of his compositions.

The Symphony in E major is his largest surviving piece and did not receive its first performance until 1989, by the Cincinnati Philharmonic Orchestra under Gerhard Samuel. It was recorded shortly thereafter, a recording I've had since 1991, listening to it occasionally, always with mixed feelings. It is a piece that always fascinates, moves, and depresses me. Let me say at once that the symphony itself is not depressing, unlike many works by Mahler, Shostakovich, and others. What depresses me is the loss of this phenomenal talent before he had had the time to mature.

A few words about the symphony's structure. It opens with a relatively short movement that presents a fabulous long-breathing tune in the brass that will resurface in the third and fourth movements. Although its debt to Wagner and *The Mastersingers* is evident, the tune has a sweeping and unpredictable quality, whose power does not diminish after several hearings. The quality of writing for the brass is phenomenal throughout. The slow movement follows also in major keys that had me thinking of Elgar and Brahms but with purely Mahlerian surges and withdrawals of emotion. The optimistic scherzo that follows is a real delight, with an upsurging melody and some woodwind writing highly evocative of Dvorak. The movement at times becomes a Ländler, a 3/4 folk dance much loved by Mahler, or even a waltz, but always preserving its optimistic outlook and its inexhaustible forward energy.

The scherzo's energy lingers on briefly in the finale, which is not only the longest but also the most brilliant of the symphony's four movements, leaving the listener truly energized and inspired. It starts with a slow introduction, during which the composer seems to be in search of a tonality and a tune. It is probably the longest section of the symphony in a minor key, and along the way, several wonderful musical ideas briefly surface and then recede. Eventually, we get the big tune, which is a chorale that owes to Brahms's First Symphony finale as much as Brahms's finale owes to the finale of Beethoven's Ninth. It is just magnificent and, to my ears, more effective than Brahms's, whose big tune originally excited me but over the years I have come to find a little tiresome. A vigorous fugal part follows before the symphony is brought to the most sublime conclusion with a re-emergence of the original theme from the first movement, embellished with copious amounts of Wagnerian Rhinewater and Magic Fires.

I must confess that every time I listen to the symphony, it leaves me truly inspired and energized. It is not just the beauty of the music, the vigour of the rhythms, the superb orchestration, and its endless evocation of themes and tunes that we all know exist without ever having heard them. This is clearly music of a young man seeking to find his voice and showing along the way a remarkable range of abilities and skills. It is also music that, while very serious in the way only Germans know and understand, is not remotely burdened by tradition—it makes joyous, imaginative, and playful use of tradition, showing that tradition need not be the graveyard of inspiration.

And yet, the young man who composed this symphony was never to move beyond his Symphony No 1. Confined to an asylum by the age of twenty-two and dead at twenty-six, Rott I would count alongside Giovanni Battista Pergolesi and Juan Crisóstomo Arriaga, as the most tragic losses to Western music. Notice how all three shared the same first name. Gustav Mahler's words stand as a worthy memorial to a unique musical figure:

> A musician of genius ... who died unrecognized and in want on the very threshold of his career. ... What music has lost in him cannot be estimated. Such is the height to which his genius soars in .. [his] Symphony [in E major], which he wrote as 20-year-old youth and makes him ... the Founder of the New Symphony as I see it. To be sure, what he wanted is not quite what he achieved. ... But I know where he aims. Indeed, he is so near to my inmost self that he and I seem to me like two fruits from the same tree which the same soil has produced and the same air nourished. He could have

meant infinitely much to me and perhaps the two of us would have well-nigh exhausted the content of new time which was breaking out for music. (Quoted in the 1989 album notes of the Gerhard Samuel recording of Rott's Symphony, Hyperion Records)

We are, of course, lucky that Mahler was to take over in his inimitable way where Rott's symphony ended. Could we imagine, however, what musical masterpieces might have emerged had Rott encountered Mahler's mature works? It is almost like trying to imagine what Mozart might have been prompted to compose had he lived long enough to hear the *Eroica*!

Koumendakis's The Murderess: The Jury Is out on a New Opera

Watching an opera or listening to a piece of music at its premiere places the audience in a difficult position. One thinks of famous premieres, notably the fiascos of the opening nights of *La Traviata*, *Carmen*, and *The Barber of Seville*. How difficult it is to listen to music that has never been heard before! Yet, it is interesting to observe our own responses as we seek to create a narrative out of what our senses feed us. I had an opportunity to attend the third performance of George Koumendakis's opera *The Murderess*, at the depth of Greece's financial and spiritual crisis in 2014, an event that has acquired even greater significance in the years that have passed. At a time when the country was suffering under the suffocating rule of the troika and its local underlings, the opera's premiere was the year's main cultural event in Athens and an occasion to reassert the existence of Greece outside the iron cage of economic realities.

The Murderess is based on a celebrated short novel of the same title by Alexander Papadiamantis (1851–1911), Greece's 'holy man of letters'. It tells the story of a village woman who kills young girls. Born to serve her parents and then a slave to her husband and later still a servant to her own children and grandchildren, Frangoyiannou develops a deep aversion for the predicament of women in her culture—her murders are motivated by a complex of pity and simmering rage, tempered by a profound despair and guilt. The novel builds a formidable psychological drama against the social panorama of Greek village life, not that much different from what it was twenty or thirty years ago.

The novel was adapted by amateur music lover librettist Yiannis Svolos before being set to music by George Koumendakis, known among other things as the music director of the opening ceremony of the 2004 Athens Olympics. The opera makes enormous demands on performers and audience. It is dominated by the mezzo-soprano performing the title role, who remains on stage virtually throughout the work's three hours. In addition to a full symphony orchestra and a complement of numerous vocal soloists, there are various instrumentalists on the stage as well as *four* choirs—a male choir playing the part of a traditional chorus of a tragedy, a female choir portraying the everyday realities of village life, a four-part traditional polyphonic ensemble of female mourners, and a huge choir of young girls feeding the protagonist's murderous fantasies.

The composer has endeavoured to stay loyal to the spirit of Papadiamantis. A large part of the music is in what the Italians call *stile concitato* pioneered by Claudio Monteverdi, an agitated recitative with florid passages, wide vocal intervals, and sudden changes of tempo and volume aimed at expressing a kaleidoscope of changing emotions. In line with Byzantine chanting tradition, much of this unfolds against a monotone sustained by the instruments or the male chorus. A large part of the music is very quiet, disrupted by sudden explosions of sound at times painful to the ear. There are various folkloric elements, but the music is generally a variant of twentieth-century tonal expressionism—the exception being the traditional polyphony and the choruses of the young girls. These last evoke traditional Greek children's songs and games but assume a demonic quality and, in their interminable repetitions, create a very high level of anxiety in the listener, presumably mirroring the mental state of the protagonist.

The leading role was taken by Eirini Tsirakidou, who gave everything she had in a performance that is engraved in my memory. She was utterly inside the role; her scenic presence, movement, facial expressions and above all the things she did with her voice were all riveting. The entire cast and the orchestra, conducted by Vassilis Christopoulos performed with total conviction, aware that this was a historic occasion. The sets and direction by Petros Touloudis and Alexandros Efklidis served the drama well—a revolving stage dominated by a three-pronged structure that became a well, a cistern, a fountain, or a hovel against a backcloth of changing mountainous imagery highly evocative of Skiathos, the site of Papadiamantis's carefully embedded drama. The rotation of the stage created a realistic impression of the protagonist's relentless flights from the village, the authorities, and her own demons that dominate the drama.

The world of the drama, in the words of the composer, is a 'world without love, a world dominated by fear, lies, hate, despair, but no love. There are no dreams, only nightmares. People are powerless, living lives without meaning in deep solitude.' This, in his view, is what links the landscape of *The Murderess* with Greece's desolation during the crisis and made it a powerful vehicle for expressing the discontents of those times. This is, however, where I felt that dramatically the opera fell somewhat short. The unremitting gloom of Papadiamantis's novel with its careful balancing act between social critique and psychological probing, did not translate so well to the stage.

The libretto is not particularly effective, remaining far too close to the novel to work dramatically. Various subplots of the novel have been excised, leaving the drama rather one-dimensional and lacking any real turning points. The murders that punctuate the novel as acts of a person driven to the limits of endurance lose much of their dramatic significance in the opera. This is especially true of the awful scene in the early part of the novel where Frangoyiannou is looking after her sickly, screaming newborn granddaughter, while the mother is trying to sleep. In the novel, the protagonist rehearses her entire life against the desperately screaming baby, a scene that tears at the soul of the reader. In the opera, the equivalent scene, which lasts more than half an hour, seemed wooden— the child silent, the protagonist uttering what sounded like mundane platitudes about the meaninglessness of life. 'All these parents, obliged to marry their daughters, five or six of them. And to provide dowries too. Every mother eats barley bread, watered by sweat, trying to find husbands for all these females.' The killing of the silent baby has nothing of the tragic pathos of the equivalent scene in the novel.

Leonard Bernstein, I believe, said that music can hugely enhance a drama. 'Think of Shakespeare's King Lear in an opera. He'd be raging as no Lear ever could rage in the spoken play: in a great bass voice, with frantic, high G-flat, with a howling chorus offstage, and ninety players helping him in the pit' (Bernstein, 1968, 289). Curiously, I found that, in this instance, music generally failed to lift or enrich the drama. It often seemed to try too hard to find the right notes, tempo, and colours to support the action but rarely revealed its emotional depth. Again, I felt that various verismo-like gestures of the librettist like, 'Drink your coffee, auntie' and

'It won't go down', would make impossible demands on any composer.

The audience warmly applauded the cast and the orchestra at the end of the performance, although there was no standing ovation. The gentleman sitting next to me, an internationally known conductor, described the work to me as 'a masterpiece' and loudly bravoed the performers. My own companions had distinctly more measured reactions after the performance, as I suspect did a large part of the audience. The applause was possibly expressing a need to celebrate the achievement of Papadiamantis and the achievement of a group of artists working together to produce a complex work of art in bleak circumstances. Maybe this was not a *succès d'estime* but a *succès de besoin*, a success growing out a desperate need to be successful in times of hardship and failure. And in this way, against the darkness that had swallowed Greece since 2009, this was a moment worth a great deal.

How difficult it is to listen to music that has never been heard before! I feel that I would need to listen to the opera at least twice again before I can express any opinion about the music with any certainty. On this occasion it failed to move me—possibly without the 'benefit' of surtitles, which emphasized the weaknesses of the libretto, it might have moved me more. But would I want to see the opera again?

Reference

Bernstein, Leonard (1968). *The Joy of Music*. London: Weidenfeld & Nicolson.

Moving My Music Library

Every lover of music with an iPod or an iPhone will be well aware of the pleasures and frustrations of iTunes, Steve Jobs's gift to humanity and a key to Apple's change from brave David of the computing industry to mighty Goliath.

Listening to music on the move was revolutionized in the 1980s when Akio Morita launched his Sony Walkman. For several decades, listening to ninety minutes of continuous music on a 'personal stereo' was as good as it got. And pretty good it was too, until the arrival of musical compression and the launch of MP3 players. My first such was a Creative Zen MP3 player, with a then awe-inspiring 64 gigabytes of memory, capable of playing the music of some 500 or more CDs, which you could readily take wherever you went. Fifteen years ago, the little Zen packed up, and I decided to upgrade to my first iPod with a colossal 160 gigabytes of memory. To do so, I had to move my music library, until then peacefully resting in the hard drive of my computer, to iTunes. It was then that my love-hate relation with iTunes started. I will spare the reader a description of my frustrations with that piece of software but will describe a recent experience of moving my iTunes library, now containing a venerable 2,472 'albums,' from one computer to another. As anyone who has undertaken this operation knows, it is riven with frustrations.

The operation was not without a hitch. I managed to transfer the albums but not the various playlists I had created. I also lost all the data on times played, date added, and so forth. No matter, the loss was small. Moving my iTunes library, however, brought to mind Walter Benjamin's bewitching little essay 'Unpacking My Library', in which he describes his feelings as he peruses his beloved books that are about to find a new home. And this made me look at some of the contents of my iTunes library, or at least what had survived in the move from one hard drive to another. Here were 2,472 albums, 1,319 artists, and 109 genres; 33,374 'songs'; 113.5 days' worth of listening; and 207.08 gigabytes worth of memory.

This is beginning to sound like Leporello's catalogue aria from *Don Giovanni*. So why not? My iTunes library contains six versions of this great opera, to my surprise all dating before 1980. This will give you an indication of my conservative musical tastes! I would rather have Giulini, Fricsay, and even the ancient Klemperer at the very end of his days, with their old-fashioned casts, harpsichords, and lack of appoggiaturas, than most of today's star conductors, with their celebrity singers, period instruments, and anxiety-provoking tempos.

And while we are on Mozart, I find in my iTunes library a total of 224 albums, with his music just behind Beethoven (239 albums) and considerably behind Bach (333). Modernists will sneer at my disregard for Stravinsky (2 albums to my shame, very rarely played), Bartok (6), et al. Of the twentieth century composers, there is only one who is truly close to my heart, much as I admire Ravel (21)—Shostakovich (64) is a composer whose music is rarely far away from my CD player or iPod.

French baroque is a favourite of mine—Couperin (34), whose harpsichord music is a constant companion; Rameau (21); Elisabeth Jacquet de la Guerre, one of my favourite female composers and a brilliant talent; Marin Marais; and others are much loved figures in my iPod library.

And performers? Among violinists, there is a spread of Oistrakhs, Heifetzs, Milsteins, Menuhins, Grumiauxs, and others. But among pianists, the spread is more uneven— my beloved Rubinstein (34) unsurpassed in Chopin (119), Ashkenazy (37), and Arrau (43). Above all, however, stands that erratic genius, Richter (102), whose music making never fails to move me (even when he plays Bartok!) even if it sometimes irritates me.

So, is there any meaning in all this? Probably not. More than 90 per cent of the music in my iTunes library was copied from my CD collection, in a piecemeal fashion. If I feel like listening to something on my iPod when I set out for a walk and it is not already there, I add it to the library. Or, if I am listening to something on my CD player that gives me great pleasure, as is now Michael Borgstede playing Couperin's 12th Ordre, I am likely to transfer it to the iTunes library once the music is finished.

But if there is no meaning in such statistics, there is maybe something of value. They offer a record of somebody's listening habits, which for someone like me is as important as reading and writing habits. And for this record, much of which disappeared earlier today when I transferred my iTunes library, I must thank Steve Jobs.

There is, however, one more factor brought to light by this little exercise. There are plenty of pieces of music that demand many different recordings, since there are so many different ways to interpret them. I find this especially with vocal music—this may explain why I have nine versions of Mahler's *Das Lied von der Erde* and only two of his First Symphony. Which opera lover would be satisfied with a single recording of *Don Carlo* or *Boris Godunov*?

The String Quartets of Dmitri Shostakovich

Dmitri Shostakovich, along with Gustav Mahler, are the two classical composers whose appeal and reputation during my lifetime has increased dramatically. Both composed massive symphonies that sought to encompass the whole of the universe, or at least the universe their formidable musical imaginations could encompass. Shostakovich's cycle of fifteen symphonies offers a fair history of Soviet Russia during the near half century (1924–1971) of their composition.

Shostakovich's other great fifteen-piece sequence, his string quartets composed between 1938 and 1974, contain more personal but equally profound insights. They are now widely recognized as musical masterpieces and have attracted the attention of several authors. I have grown to know them intimately over many years and, on a few occasions, have listened to all fifteen in chronological sequence during my walks in the countryside around Bath, experiencing their cumulative emotional effect. As a cycle, Shostakovich's string quartets strike me as being totally different from the other towering cycle of string quartets, Beethoven's. Where Beethoven with each phase of his quartet writing leaves the earlier phases behind, Shostakovich seems to return over and over to the same questions, the same musical ideas, and even the same tunes. Yet, such is his level of inspiration in these works that, having finished listening to the cycle, my main thought was to start listening to it over again.

Beethoven's cycle of quartets can be meaningfully described as a journey, a journey whose trajectory changes the artist as he makes great discoveries about the world, about himself, and about the power of his art. Not so with Shostakovich, whose second and fourteenth quartets, composed thirty years apart, inhabit essentially the same domain. In fact, the musical idea that dominates much of the second half of his last string quartet, a dirge on the persistent rhythm taa-ta-taaa, is a musical idea that we have heard already in the second and third quartets, as well as the eighth, the eleventh, and the twelfth. Can you imagine Beethoven returning to the same musical idea, say that of the magical Adagio affetuoso ed appassionato of his first String Quartet, once his musical horizons had moved on to the different range of the Cavatina of his Op. 130? And yet, this is precisely what Shostakovich does, again and again.

This then is the question—if Shostakovich's cycle of quartets cannot be described as a journey, what does it represent? Or more precisely, what is its narrative structure?

One answer that comes to mind is that the cycle can be seen as a musical conversation where the same questions, ideas, and arguments surface again and again. The notion of a conversation between four instruments is one that fits virtually every string quartet. It is also true that each of Shostakovich's fifteen contains conversation-like parts. There are hushed conversations, anxious conversations, whispered conspiratorial conversations, philosophical disquisitions, chatty gossipy conversations with knowing nods and jokes and blinks, and many more. The emotional range of these conversations varies widely. Most of them tend to be interrupted, often violently by screams and screeches, or to lead to a very different type of musical imagery.

Describing the cycle as a series of conversations simply does not do justice to the extraordinary visual imagery that each quartet evokes, something no doubt linked to Shostakovich's great skill as cinema composer. There are clear evocations of battle scenes, country fairs, wide open meadows, and bleak winter landscapes—musical evocations that recur throughout the cycle. His musical motifs tend to be rhythmically short and often punchy, melodically memorable like Beethoven's, even when they venture outside the harmonies the listener expects. Harmonically, they seem inevitable and gripping, even in the harshest dissonances. They frequently combine or morph into each other or reappear in different harmonizations, not unlike Wagner's leitmotivs.

In my own mind, various musical ideas in these works have their own titles, offering an immediate sense of recognition whenever I encounter them:

- the impudent theme (that launches Quartets 3 and 7)
- the *William Tell* overture tune (horses galloping)
- the *West Side Story* theme (Jet song)
- a bird flying high above a battlefield
- sirens—ambulances, police, and mythical
- dance of the devils
- the machine of war
- my head is a beehive
- dreaming of happiness (adagio of Quartet 10)
- meeting a ghost (dominated by pizzicati and tremolos)
- green meadows (as in the Dvorak-like opening of Quartet 6)

- police interrogation (as in Quartet 13 with the instruments tapped)
- 'alone, again' (often based on the famous DSCH theme that opens Quartet 8)
- let's drink, let's dance, let's forget
- the Hebrew theme (as in Mahler's funeral march from the last movement of *Das Lied von der Erde*)

Maybe the most persistent musical idea and one that features in nearly every quartet, is *the dirge*. Chief among them is 'the dirge of all dirges' that we first encounter in the finale of Quartet 2, the adagio of Quartet 3, the fourth movement of Quartet 8, the Elegy of Quartet 11, the lamentoso of Quartet 12, and in almost the whole of the second half of the last quartet—especially the Nocturne and the Funeral March. This is a solemn and powerful musical idea, built around the repetition of the rhythm taa-ta-taaa, the first two always in the tonic and the third sometimes in the tonic, the minor third, or elsewhere. In the last quartet, once it has taken over the proceedings, this musical idea becomes unstoppable, descending into ever more mournful depths and pulling everything else into its orbit.

One more observation about Shostakovich's quartet cycle: Many of the quartets reach their emotional peak at the quietest moment—as do some of his symphonies, most especially in the ever-fascinating Fifth's quietest passage of the Largo. Shostakovich was, of course, not the only composer to discover the highest summits when reaching for the deepest depths. One thinks of Tchaikovsky's *Pathétique*, Mahler's Ninth Symphony, as well as *Das Lied von der Erde* and even Beethoven in several of his last five quartets. What is remarkable about Shostakovich is how often he made use of this 'device'.

Shostakovich's last string quartet is an extraordinary sequence of six adagios. This, in itself, is not new. Haydn had pulled it off to great religious and musical effect in the quartet version of his choral masterwork, "The Last Seven Words on the Cross". What seems to me undeniable is that the fifteenth quartet itself marks a vortex plumbing ever deeper depths, until it eventually reaches a bottom from which there is no rising. It is not so much a conversation with death as a slow descent, a *katabasis* to Tartarus. Unlike earlier descents to the nether regions, this is one from which there is no return or resurrection; the composer has finally touched the bottom.

This, I think, gives us the answer to our original question—the narrative structure of the cycle as a whole. The cycle as a whole, with its constant return to the same themes and the same forms, in my view, has the clear shape of Greek tragedy. Every time the protagonists believe they've hit rock bottom, they discover there is worse to come; when they seek to escape their fate, through heroics, diversions, or oblivion, they find themselves more deeply entrapped; and when they see a glimmer of hope, it only serves to exacerbate the final collapse.

The Greeks did not discover any simple or encouraging solutions to what they saw with great clarity as the tragic fate of humans. Had they found a solution, they might have forestalled the various calamities that brought about the end of their civilization. In DSCH's cycle of string quartets, we encounter with the same clarity, the same inevitability, and the same power the tragic mode of human existence. This is what makes the cycle one of the profoundest musical statements of the twentieth century, perhaps the profoundest.

Callas in Aida

Aida is by no means my favourite opera. While it remains a firm favourite with the public, it has attracted some discussion recently not for its musical merits. Edward Said, for example, has deconstructed it as typical of the 'orientalist' mindset, a case of Western art appropriating cultures it does not understand or wish to understand and projecting onto them all kinds of meanings. These directly or indirectly create an idea of the 'other'—uncivilized, primitive, and infantile, unable to control his or her passions. Against this other, white man can always maintain his own identity as cultured, sophisticated, and capable of superior scientific and artistic creation.

Thomas Mann, for all his adulation of Richard Wagner, held Verdi in high regard and used the final duet of *Aida* as one of the key musical moments in *The Magic Mountain* when Hans Castorp, his young protagonist stuck in a Swiss sanatorium, discovers the power of music and spends his last days before that work's apocalyptic denouement listening to recordings on an early phonograph. Verdi's ability to turn a morbid, depressing image of two lovers dying of asphyxiation and thirst in a dark vault into something uplifting and sublime is what makes him the great genius of the Italian stage and why his operas of Egyptian princesses, Spanish gypsies, and hunchbacks in the service of medieval potentates continue to grip audiences today.

There are many excellent performances of *Aida* on record, not least by Tebaldi and Bergonzi, Caballé and Domingo, Price and Vickers. For me, however, the performance by Maria Callas recorded live in Mexico City on 7 March 1951 is a musical miracle unlikely to be repeated. The performance is available in several different 'unauthorized' (i.e. pirate) recordings, captured in very primitive sound, something anyone interested in music filters out after a few minutes. This was one of those glorious occasions when Callas, *not* my favourite singer or even my favourite soprano, could ask anything she wanted of her voice, and the voice delivered. The performance is famous for the extrapolated top E flat with which Callas crowns the conclusion of the second act, a note sung with such total security and held for so long that it alone has made the performance legendary.

This, however, is to overlook the extraordinary things Callas does with the role, the way she draws out Aida's despair, pride, and—that currently unfashionable word—nobility with no sentimentality or self-pity. Callas's Aida is no Pharaoh's slave as she is accused by her father. Nor is she a woman undone by an unsustainable romance. She is a passionate, sincere, and self-confident woman who knows from the start that there will be no happy end to her story. Callas's "O terra addio" ("Farewell to the earth") entry in the final duet is enough to melt anyone's heart and to persuade anyone of music's power to elevate and ennoble. Her duet with Taddei as Amonasro is surely terrifying in its intensity, making something of Aida's sacrifice parallel with Violetta's in *La Traviata*. Unlike so many other portrayals of Aida, here is a woman who is neither bullied nor coaxed to act against her deeper desires, a woman who, in sacrificing herself, rises to truly heroic status.

Callas's Radames is Mario del Monaco, also not my favourite Italian tenor. But this, along with Otello, must be one of his greatest recordings. Radames is a character who, like Otello and Don Jose, if sung by a lyrical tenor, becomes very easy fodder for his adversary—a pitiful hero and, hence, no hero at all. It takes the voice of a truly heroic tenor like del Monaco, Domingo, or Vickers to persuade us that Radames is a warrior, every bit the match of Amonasro, as capable of leading the Egyptian hordes as he is of demanding the release of the Ethiopian prisoners. Del Monaco's contribution to the triumphal scene is thrilling, and in the Nile duet with Callas, he tempers his tendency and does sing softly and gently. His "Morrir, si pura e bella," the only place in the opera where he leads his partner, is sung gently and with inward feeling, almost as meltingly as Bergonzi and his final words have dignity and courage.

Oralia Dominguez, who sings Amneris, was an outstanding singer who impressed me greatly with her recording of *Carmen*. Here she duets brilliantly with Callas in the early acts, never overwhelmed by the vocal phenomenon opposite her, and rises magnificently to her fourth act scene; she is so much better than various Italian mezzos who shared the stage with Callas. A clear voice, powerful, direct with no hysteria.

Taddei *was* one of my favourite Italian baritones, and here he gives a blood-curdling account of Amonasro's demonic monomania. It is difficult to think that the singer who could sing such affable Figaros, Leporellos, and Guglielmos could turn his voice into such a menacing instrument ideal for Macbeth and Scarpia and, as here, Amonasro. The orchestra and chorus of the Fine Arts Palace of Mexico City acquit themselves with much credit, as does the very skilful conductor, Oliviero de Fabritiis.

Listening to a performance of *Aida* like this, we begin to understand something of the emotional punch that Verdi's operas held during his lifetime and their catalysing effect during the *Risorgimento*. The operas have survived, and from time to time, we can experience something of the frisson they held for Italian audiences in the nineteenth century. Essentially, however, they are now museum pieces or even publicity stunts, primarily vehicles for imaginative and excitable directors always keen to shock, to question, and to provoke. It takes a miracle of a performance like this to establish the primacy of the musical language over the all-conquering commercialization and self-destructive hype of the musical stage.

The Enigma that is Mahler's Seventh Symphony

Among the great symphonists, including Haydn, Mozart, Beethoven, Schubert, Brahms, Dvorak, Bruckner, Tchaikovsky, Sibelius, and Shostakovich, I believe that Gustav Mahler stands alone in one regard. With the possible exception of the First, each and every one of the remaining eight symphonies can be meaningfully regarded as his greatest—the Fifth, widely known for its consummate adagietto; the Second, with its life-enhancing Resurrection finale; the Eighth, with its massive forces of a thousand performers; the Third, with its unmatched evocations of nature; the Sixth, unique in its apocalyptic visions; the Fourth, with its most intimate and personal utterances; and the Ninth, with its valedictory evocation of peace and tranquillity.

And what about the Seventh? I can hear you say. The Seventh, is a problem for all true Mahler lovers. A strange egg this, not so frequently performed in the concert hall, certainly nowhere near as popular as any of the above, and yet one that contains some of the composer's most profound, most intriguing, and most beautiful utterances. What then is the problem with the Seventh? In my view, the problem is really quite simple and is one I rarely see any serious music lover acknowledge—the less than inspired, indeed mediocre, quality of the finale.

Now, without a doubt, many famous composers composed some mediocre music. Shostakovich comes immediately to mind with some of the bombastic drum-beating composed at the behest of party apparatchiks. But what about Tchaikovsky? Have you ever listened to his first and fourth orchestral suites, some of his less-known operas, or indeed the perennially hyped and never failing to disappoint Second Piano Concerto? Beethoven certainly composed some routine stuff, mostly on commission, like that strange Cantata on the Death of Emperor Joseph II or the piano version of his sublime violin concerto. So too did Franz Schubert; Robert Schumann; Richard Wagner; and, with the possible exception of Chopin, virtually every other major composer.

What then is the big deal about the finale of Mahler's Seventh Symphony? The problem is that, at the end of an enormous and miraculous musical journey, the finale provides no suitable homecoming. In fact, I would go as far as to say that it ruins the journey. For a long time, I simply did not listen to it, stopping recordings at the end of the exquisite second night music. But what kind of end is this for a symphony? A highly unsatisfactory ending. I now listen to the Seventh's finale with a sense of sadness—witnessing a great mistake that can never be rectified.

Before we look at what makes the finale such a trouble spot, it is necessary to note a few things about the symphony's other movements and its overall narrative structure. The first movement is undoubtedly difficult music that takes several hearings before one can begin to understand it or emotionally connect with it. It starts in the strangest way—a slow rhythmic introduction in a distant key meant to evoke the sound of the oars as they touch the waters of a lake.

The mood is sombre; this is no ordinary boat ride but something dark and mysterious. The horn then launches a disturbed and profound melody that proves remarkably adaptable to variations and developments. It can grow, it can shrink, it can merge with other musical ideas, and it lends itself to counterpoint. This is what makes this movement quite Beethovenian—from a relatively simple motif a remarkable range of musical ideas and effects take shape.

In contrast to the opening theme that seems to constantly mutate and swallow up everything, the second theme offers a beautifully modulating upward spiral, one that strives towards the heights without ever reaching them. I have always found it far more beautiful than "Alma theme" of the Sixth Symphony. The development of the movement brings the two themes together in what I can only describe as a moment of ecstatic spiritual beauty. I find this movement a deeply moving and fascinating one, and over the years, it has emerged as one of my favourites in the Mahler canon.

The second movement is one I loved from the first time I heard it and is one of Mahler's most ingenious and enchanting compositions. It is also one of the 'stickiest'—once you start humming it, it is hard to get it out of your mind. The movement is entitled Nightmusic and derives thematically from "Revelge", one of the most harrowing songs from the *Wunderhorn* collection. The song is a terrifying march of death, punctuated by the persistent bass rhythm, a banal military drumbeat accompanying the soldiers as they march to their death in inglorious battle.

How marvellously Mahler transforms this musical idea and the banal drumbeat into a magical nocturnal landscape that combines the qualities of a serenade with those of a march! The music brings a huge range of instrumental colours as different instruments pick up the theme, always maintaining the march rhythm. You can march to the beat of this movement, from the first to the last bar! In some interpretations, the march mutates into a funeral march. But in most versions (Tennstedt, Abbado, Kubelik, and Haitink) it maintains its lyrical qualities, at times turning witty or sarcastic. Towards the end, it modulates into a Hebrew melody, an effect punctuated by some conductors' use of portamenti sliding from plaintive note to note. This is a movement of outstanding beauty, one that dispels all sense of anxiety and stress, exactly the opposite to the song that inspired it, which is laden with anxiety and gloom, with its forward movement and easy intermingling of instrumental colours. For me, it evokes less a walk in the dusk than a fantastic scene in which the creatures of the night, like those populating one of Joan Miro's paintings, come to life and begin a nocturnal procession.

By contrast, the third movement launches full of anxiety. In 3/4 time, it develops a theme used by Mahler earlier in another *Wunderhorn* song in which Saint Anthonius of Padua delivers a sermon to the creatures of the sea, which listen to him respectfully but entirely unmoved. Again, Mahler manages to completely change the mood—where the song was witty and satirical, this scherzo is dead serious, dangerous, and morbid. The music at times turns into a demonic waltz. But the theme also proves able to turn into something infinitely tender and touching. This effect is brought out to perfection in a piano version that made it an ideal choice of music, if I remember correctly, for some of the scenes in Liliana Cavani's deeply unsettling film *The Night Porter*.

Then comes the curious second Nightmusic, marked Andante amoroso, a movement played by a reduced orchestra with diminished woodwind and silent brass, except, of course, Mahler's beloved horns. The movement, the first in a major key, starts with a musical phrase that, for me, should complete a tune rather than start it, a tune already familiar from the soprano's first entrance in the finale of the *Resurrection Symphony*. It is forever associated in my mind with a Greek childhood song with the words 'Now sleep, my sweet, sweet child' that conclude each of the song's stanzas. Interestingly, Mahler develops this line with a rhythmic pulse entirely consistent with that of a lullaby but one that accompanies a sleep that alternates from peaceful to restless to, in some interpretations, full of nightmares. It is as if the father's voice, evident when the horn picks up the main melody, fails to reassure or calm the child. Unlike some commentators who see this movement as the nearest Mahler came to composing a perfect serenade, I find something troubled and unsettling in this piece but beautiful all the same. There is no doubting of the movement's *amoroso* qualities, but this is doomed, troubled, and above all interrupted love.

We now reach the point of the symphony where the finale bursts in, in glorious C major Technicolor. Mahler's intent is obvious. He wants to bring the symphony to a triumphant conclusion, like Beethoven's Fifth or, slightly less successfully, Tchaikovsky's Fifth. This is something he had tried before in his First and Fifth symphonies, neither of whose finales, in my view, is as successful as the ecstatic finales of the Second, Third, and Eighth; the valedictory one of the Ninth; the lyrical of the Fourth; or the apocalyptic one of the Sixth.

Following an eager pacesetting by the drums, the brass break in with a tune clearly inspired by Wagner's *Mastersingers of Nuremberg*. This develops into what could have been the development section of Wagner's overture, had Wagner wanted to compose a symphony, which of course he didn't. Elaborate counterpoints and fugal sections are constantly interrupted by an intrusion of numerous other themes from operetta, earlier Mahler symphonies, like the persistent and unpleasant repetition of the bowdlerized "Alma theme" from the Sixth

Symphony and even the children's chorus from Massenet's *Werther*. Most irritatingly, the tune we usually associate with "Baa, Baa, Blacksheep" seems constantly on the point of bursting forward and taking over the proceedings.

The whole movement has the character of a burlesque, compounded by a Turkish episode reminiscent of Mozart's 'Turkish music'. The music is increasingly dominated by the 'young apprentices' motif from Wagner's opera, which creates the impression that the apprentices have finally taken over the asylum and are playing all kinds of strange and tasteless tricks on the masters.

To my ears, this movement seems a total mess—and this is not the right way to say goodbye to a great symphonic work. It prompted me to reflect that, of all the musical genres, the symphony most directly demands not only a strong musical structure but also a strong narrative structure. Every symphony has to tell a story, a story that can end in many different ways but must end convincingly. Without closure, happy, sad, tragic, triumphant, romantic, the earlier episodes sink into meaninglessness and futility. Sadly, this seems to me the case with Mahler's Seventh. Confronted with the undoubted greatness of the previous four movements, the symphony's conclusion leaves the listener asking, To what end?

Comparing Mahler's Seventh with two properly unfinished symphonies, Schubert's Eighth and Bruckner's Ninth, I find myself feeling much less frustrated with the latter two. Like the *Venus de Milo* or the *Victory of Samothrace*, these symphonies have vital parts missing. We may ponder what these parts may have been, but we can still enjoy what is in front of us. With Mahler's Seventh, we are unfortunately faced with a part that is all too visible that simply spoils what we have experienced before. A pity! With a convincing finale, this could well have been Mahler's greatest symphony.

The Mysteries of Mahler's Eighth Revealed: Questions about its Musical Qualities Continue to Trouble Me

I first heard Mahler's Eighth Symphony on a vinyl recording in the 1970s, one of a set of all of Mahler's symphonies performed by the Bernard Haitink and the Concertgebouw Orchestra of Amsterdam. That was the beginning of my love affair with Mahler and the start of my Mahler Eighth problem. In the previous chapter, I wrote about my Mahler Seventh problem. But my Mahler Eighth problem is even greater. I have listened to this symphony innumerable times, in many different versions. But it rarely fulfils me. Every time I start to listen to it, I experience a beginner's enthusiasm. 'This time it will be different, I must have been missing out something over the years. This time I will finally get it!' Yet, in spite of its glorious conclusion, my experience of listening to this symphony has almost always been one of disappointment.

For many years, musicologist Stephen Johnson entertained, educated, and stimulated Radio 3 listeners with his incisive commentaries 'Discovering Music' during the intervals of classical music concerts and his erudite contributions to the

Record Review programme. He recently published a book on Mahler's Eighth Symphony, whose scope and sweep range far wider than this seminal piece of music, offering a vast panorama of musical and cultural life in Austria and Germany shortly before World War I. Could this magnificent book finally resolve my Mahler Eighth problem?

Mahler's Eighth Symphony is sometimes known as *The Symphony of A Thousand* on account of the gigantic forces required for its performance—a massive orchestra, offstage brass section, organ, two large choirs, a separate boys' choir, and eight soloists. Dedicated to Mahler's wife, Alma, the piece was premiered in Munich in September 1910 in what was a major musical and cultural event of the era. It was attended by many of the great and the good, including Thomas Mann, Stefan Zweig, Hugo von Hofmannsthal, Richard Strauss, and Anton Webern, to say nothing of assorted nobility, royalty, and sundry bigwigs. Less than a year before Mahler's death at the age of fifty, the performance was a triumph, and it established Mahler, who was already a great musical celebrity as a conductor, at the summit of the composers' pantheon.

Johnson offers a detailed account of the work, its premiere, and the public response to it and a description of the deep personal traumas surrounding its composition (death of beloved daughter, marital turmoil, and terminal illness diagnosis). He gives, too, a studious analysis of the symphony's musical structure, content, and originality. The book, however, goes well beyond this in describing the cultural and political life in Austria and Germany during the period preceding World War I, the 'belle époque'. This includes a detailed analysis of rising anti-Semitism of which Mahler was, undoubtedly, a victim despite his earlier 'conversion' to Christianity. Johnson also details the nationalist and authoritarian currents brewing as the Great War approached.

Above all, Johnson offers an incomparable insight into the music and its claim to represent something of the crowning glory in Mahler's musical output of ten symphonies and numerous song cycles. Mahler himself had no doubts about the uniqueness of this symphony, saying that his previous symphonies had been 'mere preludes' to it. He saw it as his 'gift to the nation ... a great joy-bringer', not so far away from Beethoven's message in his Ninth. He wrote, 'Try to imagine the whole universe beginning to ring and resound. There are no longer human voices, but planets and suns revolving.'

And yet! Many of us Mahler lovers have misgivings about the Eighth, which can sound grandiloquent, less musically interesting than several of her sisters, and rather short of good tunes in spite of several quotes and references to earlier works. The symphony is structured in two parts whose relation to each other is not immediately apparent. The first is a setting of the medieval hymn in Latin "Veni Creator Spiritus" ("Come Creator Spirit"), followed by a setting of the closing pages of Part Two of Goethe's *Faust*, which can be indigestible to put it mildly. It extols the eternal feminine, as different historical and mystical characters seek to raise Faust to higher planes of being and ensure his redemption.

Johnson makes a strong case that the two parts are joined by a celebration of the divine power of Eros, now sublimated as creative spirit, now as the redemptive power of love, which does not exclude sensuous and sexual love. The only dark part of the symphony, the prelude that begins Part Two before the entry of the chorus and the voices, can be seen as representing the abject state of Faust before Pater Ecstaticus, Pater Profundus, Maria Aegyptiaca, assorted choirs of angels and their kin extolling the eternal feminine finally prepare the way for his salvation.

Musically, I find a lot of this symphony 'difficult'. Part I is loud to the point of bombast. Part II starts quietly and is quite beautiful, anticipating the mood of *Das Lied von der Erde* and the Ninth Symphony, and concludes ecstatically. In the middle, there is an awful lot of loud declamatory music. To my ears, this evokes not so much revolving planets and suns as voices struggling to be heard against a barrage of choral and orchestral music. Like the *Faust* Part II text, I find much of this music indigestible, no matter how many times I listen to it.

Johnson, as ever, is superb in analysing the musical ideas of the symphony, identifying many sources of inspiration and motivic similarities with works by Beethoven, Bach, and others, the key relations between different sections and, of course, the ties between the music and the words that inspire it. He also highlights different musical themes and ideas that link this symphony to her sisters—all of Mahler's compositions are both unique and also strongly related to each other.

Composed during the crumbling of Mahler's marriage, the symphony, for Johnson, as for many others, is Mahler's attempt to win back his wife, Alma. She was at the time having an idyll, not the first one, with young architect Walter Gropius, whom she was to marry after Mahler's death. Mahler was desperately seeking to reclaim his wife, by proclaiming the power of an all-conquering love, now as a principle of solidarity, now as one of sexual ecstasy, now as the creative spirit that drives every creative artist forward. As the composer who received overwhelming acclaim by an adoring public, Mahler partly succeeded in at least temporarily reclaiming Alma's affections. But Johnson goes beyond this by making a case that Mahler was seeking to proclaim Eros against the forces of the death instinct that threatened to overwhelm him and his world, as indeed they did a short four years after the work's premiere with the onslaught of the Great War.

Johnson proves to be more sympathetic towards Alma Mahler than other commentators. In addition to the loss of her daughter, as a creative and attractive woman in her own right, she must have suffered greatly from Mahler's single-minded obsession with his art. Before her marriage to Mahler, Alma had been a composer of some talent, but Mahler was unwilling to entertain a household with 'two composers'. In a famous letter before their wedding, he said to Alma in no uncertain terms, 'From now on your only duty is to make me happy,' a statement of blinding hubris and indicative of the times in which they lived.

Johnson offers a wealth of insights into the three major works that Mahler composed after the Eighth Symphony. These include the valedictory Ninth Symphony, the mystical *and* valedictory *Song of the Earth*, and the Tenth Symphony. This is the work Mahler never completed, and in the course of its composition, he discovered his wife's infatuation with Gropius. The piece remained unperformed until musicologist Deryck Cooke prepared a performing version first performed nearly fifty years after Mahler's death. This is now mostly accepted as 'genuine' Mahler, as Mahler had left more or less detailed sketches for all five movements.

Johnson's analysis indicates convincingly that the Tenth Symphony, far from being another Mahlerian farewell to the world, was the work of a deeply traumatized man. But it was also the beginning of something new and powerful and certainly not a drift into Schoenberg's atonality. It strikes me how his discussion of what happened *after* the completion and premiere of the Eighth reveals something important about the deeper meaning of the Eighth itself. This is where my own interest in story and plot comes into its own. It is later events that prompt us to reassess the meaning of earlier ones, and this is what Johnson demonstrates, especially against those, like Leonard Bernstein, who want, indeed need, to see Mahler ending it all with a farewell. Well, the truth may be more complex, as Johnson likes to say.

A famous incident in Mahler's last year was his meeting with Sigmund Freud in Leiden, which lasted for several hours, a meeting that took place a month before the premiere of the Eighth. This encounter has generated quite voluminous literature, though much of the information about it comes from two rather unreliable sources, Alma Mahler and Freud's disciple/hagiographer Ernest Jones. We can be fairly certain that Freud, who was famously 'unmusical' (a quality he shared with Franz Kafka and something unusual for the Viennese bourgeoisie), was impressed by Mahler both as an individual of exceptional qualities and for his instinctive grasp of psychoanalysis. While the meeting was not a proper psychiatric consultation, Freud may have diagnosed that Mahler suffered from a 'Holy Mary Complex' or a mother fixation. He idealized his mother, and hence, he also idealized Alma, who he put on a pedestal ('Virgin, Mother, Queen' as we hear in Part II of the Eighth) and found it difficult to consummate his love for her. He sublimated his own sexuality in his creative process and was unable to satisfy a woman with burning sexual and emotional desires, like Alma.

An interesting part of Mahler's childhood concerns his relationship with his father. Mahler's extreme idealization of the 'eternal feminine' and his sense of being entitled to a woman whose only duty is 'to make me happy' and has no needs or desires of her own can be a consequence of a childhood fear of his father, who, Johnson informs us, could be quite a violent man, at least in his relation towards his own wife. A harsh father may prompt a five-year-old child to resolve his Oedipus complex by reaching a kind of bargain: Give up your desires of and designs on your mother. Accept that your father is where power resides. Be a good boy, do great work, and one day you will grow up and have a woman of your own who will love you unconditionally and make you happy, just like your mother did. Such a woman is not a real woman with real passions and desires of her own but the idealized 'Virgin, Mother, Queen' extolled by Goethe's Doctor Marianus and the heavenly choir.

As for Alma, I personally find it very difficult to get a firm handle. She was a woman who obviously aroused passion in many famous and creative men, like Zemlinsky, Mahler, Klimt, Kokoschka, Gropius, and Werfel; and she continues to be the subject of intense fascination. I personally find her less interesting. She must have been a very narcissistic woman and her narcissism was sustained by being the lover and wife of famous men. She must also have had very strong sexual desires and passions. And unlike Mahler, who sublimated his desires in his art, she must have found it much harder to repress them. She was obviously a victim of the gender roles of her time, without however adopting the subject position of the victim. Her escape from the Nazis and the Vichy government with her third husband, Franz Werfel, as a woman approaching sixty sounds horrendous. The deaths of her two exceptionally gifted daughters, Putzi from Mahler and Manon from Gropius, would have destroyed many other women. There is something steely about this woman. Mahler, by contrast, appears to have combined steel in surviving and even triumphing in all these endless political intrigues in Budapest, Hamburg, and Vienna with a very soft and sentimental core. Above all, he possessed what Johnson explains so well and makes this book so special—his ability to conquer pain and suffering and gain redemption through sublimation in his creative work as an artist. In this respect at least, the Eighth Symphony marks Mahler's identification with Faust both as the driven creative individual and as the man seeking redemption from unspeakable suffering.

So, let me end by returning to my Mahler Eighth problem. One of Stephen Johnson's supreme skills as a communicator in his radio broadcasts is his ability to make one listen to a piece of music with fresh ears and mind. He has prompted me to listen to music I hadn't particularly liked previously, appreciate it, and even enjoy it. He has taught me to enjoy pieces, like Nielsen's *Inextinguishable Symphony*, Strauss's *Alpine Symphony*, and (horror!) Stravinsky's *Rite of Spring*. Remarkably, I found that, in spite of its many insights, this book has not enhanced my appreciation for Mahler's Eighth. After finishing the book, I listened to six different versions of the work in very close succession. None of them gave me true joy, although I unexpectedly found Boulez's interpretation kindest to my ears. In other interpretations, I found the first movement almost insufferably loud and pretentious, the soloists' voices not so much ecstatic as nearly hysterical. I ask myself, Why exactly is Mahler celebrating Eros in this manner, just before the lights of Europe are about to go out? Is he just in denial? Could his desire to celebrate Eros and the creative spirit be doomed from the start? The second movement fared a little better, especially its ecstatic conclusion. But I still find the declamations of nearly all the soloists almost painful, as the top notes seem to stretch them nearly well beyond their reach.

Maybe these misgivings are due to a fundamental issue. Mahler, of course, did not compose the Eighth or any of his other symphonies for recording. He composed them for the concert hall. Yet I find that all the other symphonies (including the Tenth and *Das Lied von der Erde*) translate very well to recorded media. I listen to them regularly during my long walks, and I often feel truly inspired and uplifted by them, almost as if I had attended a live concert. Live performances of this symphony are always important musical events. I personally have heard it twice in the concert hall, not in particularly brilliant performances. Both times I found myself utterly thrilled and elated. Could it be that this *Symphony of a Thousand* has to be experienced live and in the concert hall to make its impact?

Meanwhile, I will continue to visit it periodically, hoping for a recorded performance that opens up the symphony's wonders to me.

Reference

Johnson, Stephen. (2020). *The Eighth: Mahler and the World in 1910*. London: Faber & Faber.

Bach's St Mathew Passion
as a Devotional Piece

Classical music lovers are well aware of the great upheaval in musical tastes brought about by the period instrument movement that started in the 1970s. This is a movement that has dramatically challenged the performing practices of many genres and has emphasized the importance of original period instruments and performing techniques, as well as a very close reading of each composer's written score down to the smallest minutiae of tempo, decorations, and so forth.

This is a movement that has spawned many good things, at its best blowing the dust off long-established ways of performing classical pieces and discovering something sharper, grittier, and faster. Nowhere has this emphasis on period performing styles been stronger than in the performing works of baroque composers and their consummate genius Johann Sebastian Bach. In performing works by Bach, whether his orchestral pieces like the *Brandenburg Concertos* or the choral masterpieces like the B minor Mass, period instrument performers have favoured faster tempos and smaller orchestral and vocal forces, sometimes thinning them down to one instrumentalist or singer per part. In the last half century, period instrument performances have come to dominate the early repertoire up to and including the large-scale works by Mozart and have increasingly encroached on the way music by later composers is performed, up to and including the romantics.

While some of the original period instrument advocates, conductors, vocalists, and instrumentalists were near fanatical in their dismissal of established tradition, their approach has now generated a tradition of its own right, a new kind of orthodoxy. As a result, many of the revered recordings of the classical repertoire, like Klemperer's Bach and Karajan's Mozart, have now come to be seen as old-fashioned and outdated, lacking in sharpness, panache, and grit. Even the emphasis on beauty of sound is now generally seen as old-fashioned, many contemporary performers mistrusting mere beauty as superficial and opting for more acerbic, staccato, and pungent sounds. Gone is the velvety vibrato and legato playing on the strings, replaced by sounds that are more provocative, sharp, and mordant.

Yet, from time to time, one listens to a performance of the old school, live or on record, that moves one deeply and prompts one to ask whether kicking out 'tradition' has been an unalloyed blessing for classical music. Such was the case when I attended a performance of Bach's supreme choral masterpiece, the *St Matthew Passion*, in Lund Cathedral on Holy Tuesday in 2014. It was performed by a group of vocal soloists and the Malmo Chamber Choir and Orchestra, a far from 'chamber-size group' whose volume and energy amply filled the cathedral's huge volumes. They were directed by their founder and music director, Professor Dan-Olof Stenlund, who has conducted the Passion more than a hundred times since 1978. What I did not know when I entered the cathedral was that this is no mere musical event in Lund but an annual ritual and a highlight in the city's cultural life.

I have heard the *Matthew Passion* in churches before, including the Bath Abbey and Norwich Cathedral, and had settled for the view that neither the acoustics nor the layout for performers and audience make a church the ideal venue for this complex and varied masterpiece. The performance in Lund altered my view. Sitting very near the front, I had a perfect view of the performers, and the acoustics, which involved a four-second reverberation, worked mostly to the music's advantage. The cathedral's unique architectural features accorded to perfection with this summit of musical baroque.

The work's start brought about a totally unexpected experience. The conductor entered with no applause and stood at the podium, and the bells of the cathedral sounded for a good two minutes. The bells then fell silent, and a truly primal drone emerged from the orchestra as they opened the huge chorus "Kommt, ihr Töchter, helft mir klagen," the orchestra's four double basses creating an effect I have never heard before. The entrance of the vibrant double choir was nothing short of breathtaking, the antiphonal effects working magnificently.

The work was sung in Swedish, a practice I find entirely acceptable. As a long-standing admirer of Sir David Willcocks's recording in English, I feel that, in this work, it helps greatly when the performers are intimate with the words they are singing. As you can imagine, this was not a period instrument or 'historically informed' performance; it would be fair to describe it as *devotional* from beginning to end, and hence, understanding the words for performers and audience is vital. Mellow sounds, generally slow or very slow tempos, and a total commitment to creating a religious feeling even for the non-religious were the performers' guiding spirit, determined as they were to do an annual ritual the justice it deserves.

What does 'devotional' mean and how does it contrast to currently fashionable performing 'styles'? I suppose that, in the first instance, it implies that performers and audience do not expect the performance to be judged in the same way the most recent recording by star conductor X and his or her orchestra Y and choir Z are judged. A devotional performance is one that is not subject to changing fashions; nor does it seek to thrill with new effects. It gains its power through total conviction in what it does, through repetition and unwavering confidence in the rightness of its approach. It does not seek to surprise or even to please but to communicate profound and incontestable feeling. This was undoubtedly the approach of conductor Dan-Olof Stenlund, who created overpowering effects, especially in the big choral moments like the chorus "So ist mein Jesus nun gefangen—Laßt ihn, haltet, bindet nicht!" with soprano and alto and the colossal fugue for double choir that follows it, "Sind Blitze, sind Donner in Wolken verschwunden".

The sound of Bach, like a powerful river that sweeps everything along its majestic way, came to my mind repeatedly while listening to this wonderful performance. As I noted, devotional performances are not to be judged by conventional aesthetic criteria, and audiences easily forgive the odd mistake or mistiming. Yet the Lund audience was knowledgeable and demanding. I had several discussions with my neighbours during the beginning, the end, and the lengthy interval about the quality of the performance, and they showed a keen critical spirit. Several noted that those of the arias delivered from the back of the orchestra did no justice to the singers, and this too was my view. I should note, therefore, the tireless evangelist of Greger Erdös, who looked like Jussi Björling and sounded like Hughes Cuenod. In addition to his duties as evangelist, he sang the two long tenor arias with a voice that cut through the church's huge expanses with laser-like precision (in part, because he stood throughout at the front of the orchestra). The noble Christ of Per Fernesten and the radiant soprano

Malin Landing also deserve special praise, as do the divine flute sounds, not my favourite instrument, produced by the flutists throughout the performance. But the evening belonged to the choir of some eighty singers who gave their all, whether as hysterical crowds, devoted worshippers, or ultra-competent musicians delivering fugues of immense complexity and depth. All this was a great achievement for a group that included some teenagers as well as white-haired veterans who might have sung the same work in the 1970s.

The performance ended four hours after it had started with a breathtaking account of the final chorus "Wir setzen uns mit Tränen nieder", which had me thinking about all of the world's sufferings and troubles, sung with great dramatic effect to bring this ritual to a worthy close. But the ritual was not over as the final C minor chord faded out. There was no applause. Total silence, broken an instant later by the sound of the cathedral bells to announce that something wonderful and great had been accomplished one more year.

And a small note to finish this chapter. At 8, 9 and 10 p.m. during the performance, the cathedral's famous astronomical clock struck hourly with a series of thuds that seemed remarkably like the sound of a hammer hitting nails. The performers continued their remarkable work entirely unperturbed, making this a deeply moving musical experience. It was also a moving religious experience even for an atheist like me.

Opera and Politics

Opera today is widely seen as an elitist art form. Public subsidies for opera, at least in England, attract regular criticism. It was not always like this. Starting with the first private theatre built in Venice in 1637, opera was aimed at different social classes. Mozart's *Magic Flute* was composed for a public that resembled more the audience of a contemporary pop concert than a group of snobbish cognoscenti. During the golden era of Italian melodrama, it was not uncommon to hear a recently premiered opera's best tunes played by street organ grinders. Even more so, there was a time when opera was capable of launching revolutions. In 1830, following a performance of Auber's grand opera *La Muette de Portici* in the Theatre de la Monnaie in Brussels, a crowd stormed the local courthouse, setting off the revolution that led to Belgian political independence. The opera that so stirred the passions of Belgian patriots was about a failed revolution in Naples in 1647. In it, the rebel leader, Masaniello, becomes horrified by the brutality of the mob, is denounced as a traitor, and is finally murdered by his own followers.

Opera is a political genre, capable of depicting and questioning political events in highly illuminating ways. Revolution is not an uncommon theme for opera. Nor indeed are wars with victories and defeats, enslavement and liberation, peace treaties, state marriages, exiles and public executions, conspiracies, political assassinations, state visits, succession struggles, dictatorship, democracy, and many other political phenomena. Over its history of nearly four hundred years, from Claudio Monteverdi's *Incoronazione di Poppea* (1643) to John Adams's *Nixon in China* (1987), opera has regularly sought to depict, criticize, and comment on power and oppression in every conceivable context. Opera has shown a considerable versatility in engaging with the great public issues of different eras—from the rise of the bourgeoisie in Mozart's *Nozze di Figaro* (1786) to Mark-Anthony Turnage's treatment of media-fed celebrity culture in *Anna Nicole* (2011), a dramatization of the life of the American model and television personality. State politics, family feuds, class politics, racial politics, religious politics, and gender politics have never been out of its sights.

The subjects chosen by opera composers reflect the political realities and anxieties of their time. Written before the failure of the 1848 revolutionary efforts in Italy, Verdi's early operas, with their rousing choruses and great exaltations of patriotism, expressed the ideals of Italian unification and independence. The slogan 'Viva Verdi' came to stand for 'Viva Vittorio Emanuele Re D'Italia' (Long Live Victor Emmanuel, King of [unified] Italy). Verdi himself, 'the voice of the Risorgimento' served in Italy's first national parliament, and his funeral cortege in 1901 was followed by a crowd of some 300,000. His German rival, Richard Wagner, actively supported the unsuccessful Dresden Revolution in 1849 and was forced to live for eleven years in exile. Long after his death, his music dramas with their powerful evocation of a heroic Nordic past provided a vibrant ingredient of Nazi ideology. The connection between Wagner's music and Nazi politics still arouses great passions. Wagner was a notorious anti-Semite and racist, and his operas are not performed in Israel to this day.

The political power of opera was recognized early by various censors who sought to control and tame it. Mozart, Verdi, and Wagner, probably the three greatest operatic composers, repeatedly fell afoul of censors, as did virtually every major operatic composer of the nineteenth century. Many famous operas exist in different versions as a result of their composers' attempts to meet, to evade, or even to resist the demands of censorship. Dmitri Shostakovitch's opera *Lady Macbeth of the Mtsensk District* prompted a denunciation by the Communist Party newspaper *Pravda* in 1936 sometimes attributed to Stalin himself as 'an ugly flood of confusing sound ... a pandemonium of creaking, shrieking and crashes' warning that 'it might end very badly' for the composer. The work was banished for some thirty years and left Shostakovich living in fear of arrest and execution for much of the rest of his life.

Opera is a political phenomenon, not merely in its content but in the passions that it arouses and the political processes it sets in motion. This is true even today, when it is no longer capable of launching revolutions but can be the topic of acrimonious debates. Individual opera productions are constantly sparking bitter disputes over whether they insult public mores or artistic tastes. Even more significantly, the question of whether the state should be subsidizing an elitist art form in which the large majority of the population has no interest is never far from the public agenda.

The staging of an opera is itself a political process, involving many competing interests, including those of the composer, the producer, the conductor, and the theatre director, to say nothing of various temperamental singers and the multitudes of support workers—chorus members, orchestral players, technicians, and stagehands. Indeed, there have been several operas, including by Mozart and Richard Strauss, *about* the staging of an opera and associated conflicts and complications. For all the accusations of operatic elitism or maybe *because* of them, the BBC series *The House*, documenting Jeremy Isaacs's leadership of London's Royal Opera House in 1995, attracted more than four million viewers. They were drawn to it largely by what seemed like the political shenanigans and intrigues of overstretched leadership, financial mismanagement, constant technical and human problems, embittered staff, and capricious prima donnas.

The four chapters that follow look closely at two of opera's psychological and political dimensions. We first look at the insights opera brings to collective or mass psychology through the device of many individuals singing together in a chorus. We then look at opera's insights into leadership psychology through a discussion of musical portraits of three powerful historical figures.

The Chorus and the Psychology of Collective Followership

Singing together in religious, political, or even sporting events stirs up powerful emotions in most of us. Through the collective voice of the chorus, opera is able to represent collective actions and sentiments of multitudes in their complexity and force, augmenting the emotional and political content of the text through music. Operatic choruses can show groups of people acting as rebellious mobs, as disciplined fighting units, as confused and needy subjects, as patriotic crowds thirsting for freedom, as merrymaking gatherings, as debating assemblies, as religious congregations, and many others besides. Indeed, there are several major operas in which the chorus is a major character in the storyline or even the protagonist. 'It is an opera not of heroes and heroines, but of crowds and armies,' Bernard Shaw wrote astutely about Rossini's *William Tell*, something that can be said about several other works as well.

Operatic composers were not, of course, the first to use a chorus in giving voice to shared feelings and attitudes. The chorus in Greek tragedy was usually a group of men or women witnessing events and actions on the stage and offering a critical commentary on the characters, the situations they faced, and their actions. Singing choirs are a central part of

Western ecclesiastical tradition, where polyphonic music, with its dissonance and chromaticism, was reluctantly accepted by the Church as a means of praising God, reaching its own apotheosis in the great oratorios of Bach and Handel. The chorus also plays a major part in some large symphonic works, starting with Beethoven's Ninth Symphony. It is in opera, however, where it demonstrates its full dramatic potential by actually driving the drama forward and inviting the audience to share its own predicament and judge its actions.

Consider, for example, the famous chorus "Va, Pensiero" from Verdi's *Nabucco*, the music spontaneously sung by the crowd that followed his funeral cortege more than half a century later. Exiled from their home to Babylon, oppressed, and exploited, the Hebrew slaves are lamenting their fate in verses like, 'Oh, my fatherland, so beautiful and lost! Oh, remembrance, so dear and so ill-fated.' What gives these words their great power and makes them utterly unforgettable is, of course, the music. They are sung in hushed unison by the chorus to one of Verdi's sweeping melodies that carries everything along. The music's almost unbearable nostalgia and yearning transcend individual differences to become part of a shared experience and a shared ideal, one that immediately reaches out to the audience. Between the world of biblical Jews, even in the Verdian reimagining, and the Italians' messy political struggles for independence, the gap is huge. And yet, Verdi's music brings the two together by juxtaposing an actuality of lack and oppression with a vision of freedom and independence.

"Va, Pensiero" was the first of many patriotic choruses that established Verdi as a significant political figure of his age. Another example from a year later is the chorus "O Signore dal tetto natio" from *I Lombardi alla prima Crociata*. It is worth noting that, in turning Shakespeare's *Macbeth* into an opera, Verdi sought to compensate for the omission of several dramatic episodes of the original, by composing substantial choral parts, including the chorus "Patria oppressa" sung by Scottish exiles echoing the sentiments of the Hebrew slaves and, if anything, bleaker and more desolate. This chorus was substantially enhanced in the revisions that Verdi carried out for the Paris production of the opera in 1865, where he also concluded the drama with a victory chorus celebrating the death of the tyrant and the end of oppression. It is the presence of the chorus throughout the opera that highlights the political character of the Macbeths' crimes, and its final celebration conveys the political message that tyrants do not last forever. The last word belongs neither to the dying tyrant nor to the new leaders; it belongs to the people.

The chorus in several of Verdi's early operas acts as a leaderless mass, even if a leader (like the priest Zaccaria in *Nabucco* and Macduff and Malcolm in *Macbeth*) at some point steps in to lead them. In contrast to the tyrants they oppose, these figures are dwarfed by crowds of followers they lead; it is not the leaders but, rather, the followers who eventually ensure that good will prevail against evil and that the mass of humanity will hold tyrants to account. In his early works, which were as much an expression of political aspiration as of purely musical values, Verdi offered an idealized view of the crowd driving historical events that may be seen as one-dimensional or simplistic. It is worth remembering, however, that, in the aftermath of the French Revolution, many intellectuals, such as Edmund Burke and Hippolyte Taine, had come to view revolutionary crowds as 'band[s] of cruel ruffians and assassins, reeking with … blood' (Rudé 1959, 2) or at least as rabble. This view can be found in numerous operas, including in *La Muette de Portici* that launched the Belgian Revolution and Benjamin Britten's *Peter Grimes*; and Verdi's idealization of the crowd stands as an important corrective.

A different depiction of the masses is presented in Mussorgsky's opera *Boris Godunov*. The work is a sprawling political panorama of events in Russia during the doomed reign, from 1598 to 1605, of Boris Godunov. The tsar assumed power following the death, possibly by assassination, of the legitimate heir, ten-year-old Dmitry, who had been placed under his protection. The opera exists in several versions, involving a number of scenes, some public and grand, some private and intimate. It has a huge cast of characters, including the tsar and his children; monks, chroniclers, and a pretender to the throne; a variety of boyars and noblemen; a Jesuit priest and a Polish princess; various policemen and frontier guards; a simpleton or holy fool; and, above all, the people. The chorus is a vital part of this drama. As it frequently does for Verdi, here too the chorus represents, above all, the suffering people—in this instance, the people of Russia during the period referred to as the 'time of troubles'. Unlike Verdi's choruses, however, the chorus assumes many different and highly differentiated forms. It appears now as a rent-a-mob pleading with Boris to become their king, now as a hungry and desperate crowd, now as a gang of unruly and callous street children, now as a riotous throng quarrelling among themselves, now as a mob thirsting for blood, and now as an enduring and noble mass of humanity praying for a better future.

A particularly brilliant portrait of the people emerges in the revised version of the opera's final scene, known as the revolution scene. It starts in the pandemonium of a revolution depicting an anarchic mob, including men, women, and children, who have captured a local nobleman. They are baiting him and beating him and are about to torture and kill him. They're interrupted by the arrival of two itinerant vagabond monks who announce the coming of a new tsar, the False Dmitry, and denounce the crimes of Boris Godunov.

125

They, in turn, are followed by two Jesuits, who are captured by the mob, which is ready to hang them. At the crucial moment, the pretender and his predominantly foreign retinue arrive on the stage. Urged by the vagabond monks, the mob immediately acknowledges him as their new tsar. He, in turn, frees the captive nobleman and asks the crowd to follow him onto Moscow to seize power. They all exit the stage, leaving the holy fool alone to lament the sufferings of the people; they have now embarked on another ill-fated adventure under a different doomed leader.

In the course of the barely twenty minutes that this scene lasts, we see the crowd first as an anarchic but differentiated mob lusting for revenge—all energy and no direction or plan. They then come under the influence of two opportunists who egg them on, only to embrace their new ruler, even though his first action is to deprive them of their prey. Their cries of 'Glory, Glory' are almost identical to those with which they had greeted his predecessor, bringing the plot full circle to the earlier scene when the same people were celebrating Boris's coronation. For all its political insights, opera rarely offers any conclusive answers to the burning political issues of justice, equality, and freedom that preoccupy every political society. At its best, like ancient Greek tragedy, it raises our understanding and sensitivity to these issues and, in some cases, may stimulate a political will, individual, or collective to act and confront them.

Reference

Rudé, G. (1959). *The Crowd in the French Revolution*. Oxford: Oxford University Press.

Operatic Portrait 1: Verdi's Simon Boccanegra

In addition to the power of the chorus to express collective wishes and fantasies, opera can offer illuminating portraits of leaders and their relationships with their followers. Operatic rulers range far and wide—heroic, tyrannical, benevolent, flippant, wise, guilt-ridden, magnanimous, punitive, loving, deranged, enlightened, ambitious, depressed, narcissistic, paranoid, illegitimate, and so forth. They can be terrifying or merely ridiculous. Mustafa in Rossini's *L'Italiana in Algeri* is a good example of the latter, spiced with ill-hidden racist prejudices and xenophobia. They can be male or female; in fact, among the most villainous characters in all operas, one finds queens or princesses, like the Queen of the Night in Mozart's *Magic Flute*; the lead female characters in Verdi's *Nabucco* and *Macbeth*; and the title roles in Rossini's *Semiramide*, Strauss's *Salome*, and Puccini's *Turandot*. They can be triumphant or punished by their karma; and usually in opera, cruel and unjust leaders pay with their lives. Some remarkable exceptions include Nero and Poppea in Monteverdi's *Incoronazione*. As with all drama, the same leader can be portrayed in many different ways by different interpreters in different productions—as we saw in our earlier discussion of Verdi's Otello, who can be portrayed as noble warrior, jealous husband, deracinated alien, and so forth.

Rulers in opera, even idealistic ones, suffer and usually fail in their missions. To be sure, most operatic rulers are kings and potentates, tyrants and occasionally democratically elected politicians, rather than princes or conventional heroes, roles generally assigned to even more doomed characters. In the few occasions when opera places an ostensibly charismatic leader, like Joan of Arc, Moses, or Alexander the Great centre stage, the result scarcely highlights the character's charisma, in the way, for example, that Bach does so successfully in his portrayal of Christ in his two settings of the Passion. Instead, charismatic leaders, when they feature in opera, tend to emerge either as conflicted and tormented beings or as rather monochromatic characters on autopilot with destiny.

Opera at its best, with its ability to invest words with conscious and unconscious significance afforded by music, opens windows into the psychology of leaders. It can explore and expose in detail their emotions—ambivalence, confusion, doubts, regrets, disappointments, hopes, and despair, to name just a few. It can reveal inconsistencies between desires and actions and discontinuities between intentions and outcomes. More specifically, opera can reveal sharply the leader's inner conflicts and torments that are rarely discussed in public, as well as the distance between a leader's inner state of mind and his or her public pronouncements and displays. This is the case with the three leadership portraits discussed here, all dating from the latter part of the nineteenth century and all dealing with real historical personages from several centuries earlier. All three leaders in question lived in times of strife, war, and rebellion. And their operatic portraits display considerable psychological but also political complexity and depth.

In Verdi's *Simon Boccanegra*, the eponymous character, a former pirate, aided by two corrupt conspirators, is elected doge of Genoa in a successful attempt by the plebeians to seize power from the aristocracy. The opera's tortuous plot is rife with conspiracies, conflicts, alliances, and betrayals, at the political, family, and personal levels. But behind the various machinations, deaths, curses, reunions, and reconciliations, we have a magisterial portrait of a leader, whose legitimacy at the start of the drama is questionable, but who, in the course of it, rises to considerable stature and authority as he strives to maintain the unity and harmony of the state in the face of rebellion and strife. The political motivations of the doge are closely intertwined with his most private feelings; in the course of the opera, we see him regularly deflected from his political goals because of his love for his daughter.

At the heart of the opera is a uniquely powerful scene, added by Verdi some twenty-four years after the work's premiere, in which Boccanegra stands up to a rebellious crowd invading the council chamber. Plebeians and patricians throw a variety of accusations and recriminations at each other, and intermittent fighting erupts, which Boccanegra effectively quells with a message of peace inspired by Petrarch. Throughout the opera, Boccanegra is portrayed as someone who seeks to heal class divisions in the light of conspiracies and betrayals (which also afflicted the historical Boccanegra throughout the two periods of his dogeship). At the opera's desolate end, Boccanegra, reconciled with his patrician foe, dies, poisoned by the man who had orchestrated his ascent to the throne. Before he dies, and as the crowd is already mourning his demise, he anoints the young patrician who had earlier sought to kill him as his successor. The omens for his successor are clearly bleak.

Anger and intimidation are in this leader's repertoire as he is portrayed in the opera. His anger is indeed terrifying, and it has to be terrifying if it is to control the forces of chaos and anarchy that he faces, in the manner of a true Machiavellian ruler for whom maintaining the cohesion of his state is a supreme responsibility.

But this is also a leader capable of displaying great generosity, magnanimity, and love, aware that neither peace nor harmony can be built through tortures and executions. This ecumenical empathy is vastly amplified by Verdi's magnificent music; it is surely not a coincidence that Simone's most memorable musical utterance occurs during the council chamber scene. This leads to a majestic ensemble in which the doge's passionate appeal for brotherhood enables the other characters, patricians and plebeians, allies and enemies, at least publicly, to join him in expressing similar feelings, even if they do not sincerely hold them.

Opera thrives in presenting leaders in situations of crisis, strife, and conflict. The notion that leaders may enjoy a quiet and peaceful time is instantly dispelled by a casual look at any operatic text, even before one listens to the music to which it is set. Leaders are called to face conflict. Sometimes this may not be of their own creation, but it is usually their own actions, knowingly or unknowingly, that unleash conflicts without which there is no drama. One aspect of conflict starkly revealed by opera is how easily interpersonal and family conflicts turn into political conflicts and vice versa. Conflict lies at the heart of leadership. And even when passionately and sincerely pursuing peace like Simon Boccanegra, a leader is someone willing to fight and struggle for his or her beliefs and interests; a leader constantly lives with conflict and its unpredictable consequences. Opera amply confirms the statement by leading political theorist James MacGregor Burns that, 'Leaders, whatever their professions of harmony, do not shun conflict; they confront it, exploit it, ultimately embody it' (Burns, 1978, 39).

Reference

Burns, James MacGregor. (1978). *Leadership*. New York: Harper & Row.

Operatic Portrait 2:
Verdi's King Philip II

Maintaining the cohesion of the state in the face of religious war and rebellion is also essential to understanding another major leader as portrayed in opera, Philip II of Spain. He is a central character in Verdi's *Don Carlos*, which was inspired by Friedrich Schiller's eponymous drama. Philip is a less sympathetic character than Boccanegra, willing to send rebels and heretics to their death in defence of his realm, to abandon his only friend and ally to the Inquisition, to cheat, to spy on and bully his wife and her retinue, and eventually to sacrifice his rebellious son in the interest of the state. In the hands of a lesser composer or a less politically shrewd composer, Philip would emerge as a mere brute of a man or just a melodramatic villain. What makes Verdi's portrait of Philip so compelling and instructive is, firstly, the dramatic situations in which the composer places him (and these owe a lot to Schiller) but, more importantly, the music that Verdi composed for Philip's deep and authoritative bass voice.

Unlike Boccanegra, Philip has no direct problems with his legitimacy. He is the rightful monarch, the son of Charles V of the Holy Roman Empire. And in addition to the Iberian Peninsula, he rules many parts of Italy; central Europe; and, of course, Flanders, where he faces a bitter religious war and rebellion. He doesn't appear until a good hour into the opera and thereafter assumes centre stage. We first encounter him brutally dismissing the queen's lady in attendance for disobeying his orders. We then see him in a heated political argument with the idealistic Marquis de Posa on the value of freedom and peace, in which Philip defends the use of naked force in defence of the realm. At this point, the orchestra bursts in a cacophonous explosion of sound, indicating both the ferocity of the force and the composer's questioning its legitimacy. Yet, the argument closes mysteriously with the king taking his opponent into his confidence with the words:

> Your proud gaze has penetrated deep into the
> heart of my throne;
> Learn then the anguish and grief inside a head
> Weighed down by the crown;
> Look now at the royal palace
> And the anxiety that pervades it.
> Unhappy father, husband unhappier still.

In the next act, we see Philip dismissing the pleas for mercy of Flemish deputies; confronting Carlos, his son, who draws a sword against him; and celebrating the public burning of heretics. We then meet Philip in his royal study after a sleepless night, lamenting a loveless marriage, a palace full of traitors, and conspirators with eyes on the throne and a life that will only find rest in the black vault of the Escorial. This soliloquy, which, in many performances, ends with the monarch weeping privately, is rendered to the greatest music that Verdi composed for the bass voice (and possibly for any voice) and is followed by another political encounter. This time, Philip meets the indomitable figure of the Grand Inquisitor, who demands the death of Posa, the only man that Philip can trust or for whom he has any affection. The encounter between state and church, vocally depicted through the struggle between two bass voices, can only be described as terrifying. The king's final words, musically diving from the highest note of his voice to the lowest, leave no doubt as to the outcome of the struggle:

> Thus, the throne will always
> Bow in front of the altar!

In the rest of the opera, united, the throne and the altar bring about the death of the idealist Posa; quell another crowd rebellion led by Carlos; and, in the final scene, preside over the demise of Carlos himself, although Verdi and his librettist departed from Schiller here, allowing for some ambiguity concerning the prince's actual end.

As a potent piece of political music drama, *Don Carlos* offers a portrait of a leader who is lonely, suspicious to the point of paranoia, brutal, and autocratic. He is strongly reminiscent of Plato's depiction of tyrants whose need to dominate stops them tasting 'true freedom or friendship'. Philip's isolation is near total, but so too is his courage in the face of opposition and adversity. Although never a sympathetic character, Philip emerges as a believable, three-dimensional person with a single mission—to maintain the unity of his empire at all costs. To this end, he is willing to sacrifice his son; his only friend; and, of course, any claim to personal happiness. Sacrifice is a key aspect of leadership, one that features in countless operas, from Mozart's *Idomeneo* to Wagner's *Walküren* and in innumerable religious texts, not least the Christian New Testament. Sacrifice is the sine qua non of leadership. In the first instance, leaders must sacrifice any claim to privacy and tranquillity for themselves and for their families too. Leaders are often called to make other sacrifices—to sacrifice their dreams, their consciences, their principles, or even their followers. Sacrifice underpins the leader's isolation and is also the hallmark of the leader's power, a power whose failure turns leaders themselves into sacrificial victims.

If leaders making sacrifices or being sacrificed themselves are not rare in opera, the image of a supreme leader like Philip II weeping away from the public eye is a rare and very powerful one. It is certainly an image that haunts Thomas Mann's (1968) young Tonio Kröger. And when a public figure of considerable authority, such as a politician, a judge, or even a teacher, is seen crying, the effect can be overwhelming and unpredictable, as demonstrated by Margaret Thatcher when leaving office or George W. Bush when awarding a posthumous medal to a dead serviceman. To see a person in authority cry, and if the tears are seen to be genuine rather than manufactured for effect, destroys the leadership mystique and lays bare the unconscious fantasy of the leader as someone above others, one who is not affected by the same afflictions as ordinary mortals. Such then is the power of the operatic portrait of leader. Opera can bring leaders and their vulnerabilities close to the audience in a way that public pomp and circumstance seek to conceal.

Reference

Mann, Thomas (1968). *Tonio Kröger*, (ed. E. M. Wilkinson, 2nd edn). Oxford: Blackwell.

Operatic Portrait 3:
Mussorgsky's Boris Godunov

Unlike Philip II, in most productions we do not see Boris Godunov crying. But we do see him collapse twice psychologically in the course of Mussorgsky's sprawling political panorama. The first time, he is undone by his courtier Vasiliy Shuisky's description of the killing of the ten-year old Dmitry, the legitimate heir to the throne. Later, and as the drama approaches its denouement, he meets the elderly chronicler Pimen, who describes a dream of the murdered child and a subsequent pilgrimage to his grave, something that precipitates Boris's final collapse and death. What we witness in these two scenes is a ruler in the grip of utter terror leading to his physical, spiritual, and psychological unhinging. Witnessing such terror has a mesmeric effect on the audience and destabilizes another aspect of the leadership mystique, the fantasy of the leader as all-powerful and fearless in the face of extreme adversity. The effect is augmented by the breakdown of the musical line and the performer lapsing into something more akin to talk, as if the musical language has reached its limit in the face of abject horror, overpowering guilt and blind panic, emotions we rarely witness in a ruler and are even hard to imagine.

In another memorable scene, we see Boris meeting the holy idiot or simpleton (*yuródiviy*) outside Saint Basil's Cathedral. The last person to remain in front of the Tsar when a desolate crowd has melted away, the idiot accuses him of having blood on his hands, a charge that goes unanswered. This scene brings the supreme leader face to face with the lowest of his subjects and destabilizes another facet of the leader mystique by reversing the archetypal scene of meeting God on the Day of Judgement. Here, it is the lowly subject who passes judgement on the supreme leader, drawing the leader outside the rehearsed routines of protocol and ceremony and inviting us to judge him in a more authentic light. Whereas elsewhere in the drama, the people, when confronted with overbearing power, stay silent, here it is the monarch who stays silent in the face of the most extreme accusation that precipitates yet another crisis to his claim to legitimacy. Like Boccanegra and Philip II, Boris finds himself in total isolation. But unlike them, the outer crisis he faces unleashes an inner crisis from which he will not recover.

All three leadership portraits we examined here present rulers who are isolated, who face challenges to their legitimacy; who are constantly fighting conspirators and traitors undermining their rule; and who are governing countries torn by social strife, war, and divisions. They all are greatly concerned with maintaining the unity of their state, and to different extents, they care for the welfare of their subjects. They are all prepared to make sacrifices and are willing to sacrifice their peace of mind in the interest of the state. They wield considerable power, and yet they discover that this power is regularly foiled by religious and other institutions, and it gives them no carte blanche in attaining their objectives. They all find that, between their actions and the outcomes of these actions, there is an insurmountable gulf. All three carry heavy burdens. They all three suffer.

What makes these portraits particularly compelling is that, in addition to their public roles, we meet all three of them in intimate family situations. Boccanegra is reunited with a long-lost daughter after many years of separation, while Philip is engaged in a long-standing battle with his idealistic son and heir. Boris maybe faces the most harrowing domestic situation of the three. In one of the tenderest moments of the drama, we encounter him playing with his son and his daughter, a truly dedicated and loving father. Yet, as he gradually comes apart, he realizes he cannot vouchsafe the happiness of his beloved children; indeed he cannot ensure their survival in the days that will follow his demise.

These intimate aspects of leadership, in all their complexity and ambivalence, are ones we rarely glimpse in scholarly literature. In opera, on the other hand, they provide a powerful counterweight to the leader's public duties. Family life, far from being an irrelevant distraction, turns out to be every bit as political as the public arenas. It is a conjugal dispute with his wife, whom he believes unfaithful, that leads Philip to a paroxysm of anger, prompting Posa to tell him:

> Sire, half of the world is in your power
> In such a vast empire,
> Are you the only person you cannot rule over?

Two further aspects of leadership that are greatly highlighted by opera are the leader's propensity to punish disobedience and to reward loyalty—both of these are liable to abuse. Punishments meted out by leaders can be unduly harsh, while rewards for loyalty easily turn into recipes for nepotism and flattery. Indeed, while emphatically focusing the stage lights on the faces of leaders, opera rarely idealizes them. On the contrary, with the exception of celebratory or sycophantic works, opera is suspicious of the idea of charismatic leaders who, through force of personality or gift of grace, can sweep all obstacles aside and lead their followers to a promised land.

Operatic leadership is ineffably linked to ambition, even when a leader assumes power reluctantly, as in the cases of Boccanegra and Boris. Ambition can make leaders attractive to followers. Yet, it quickly becomes a double-edged sword. It can help leaders assume great power and make them hugely popular with followers; it can also enable them to endure unpopularity and adversity. In the majority of cases, it also leads to their downfall, something that can be observed daily in our times with leaders of business organizations, international bodies, public sector organizations, and political parties, as demonstrated by the tribulations that afflicted several of the UK's recent prime ministers. Opera, therefore, consistently highlights the dark side of leadership, poignantly and pointedly indicating that the same qualities that raise leaders to great heights, their ambition, self-confidence, eloquence and decisiveness, also account for their shortcomings. This, maybe, is the most important lesson from opera, as it is from tragic drama—the same qualities that account for a leader's triumphs also account for his or her downfall.

This may be the most important lesson that opera affords us on the topic of leadership. Great figures make for powerful drama, especially if we can observe them and compare their actions on the large political stage as well as in intimate contact with their close associates and their families. Opera can highlight the needs of the people as followers through powerful choruses and large multitudes acting and singing in concert on stage, emphasizing their propensity to turn to a 'strongman', especially in times of stress and uncertainty. In most such cases, leaders, successful at first, are more liable to disappoint than to meet the exaggerated expectations and hopes of their followers. Early miracles and triumphs are generally preambles to calamities and misfortunes.

Musical Legends

A friend of impeccable musical taste took me to task recently for referring to Soviet conductor Yevgeny Mravinsky as 'legendary'. What makes a figure legendary? she asked. In these days of media hype, does popularity turn any flash-in-the pan celebrity into a legend? By coincidence, at about the same time, I heard Antonio Pappano refer to Luciano Pavarotti as 'legendary' in his series of documentaries, *Voices*. We classical music lovers are undoubtedly given to referring to some of our idols as legendary. Does the word have any meaning, or should we give it up as hollow term used when every other type of hype has been exhausted

Obvious things first. Someone can be legendary without being world-famous or a celebrity. It is not essential to be well known in order to be legendary. A small group of connoisseurs can treat someone or something as legendary, even if the wider public have no idea about it. A closed circle of connoisseurs is more likely to spawn a legend than the open reaches of the mass and social media. Mass media, as well as social media today, are just as likely to relish the demolition or debunking of a legend as the creation of one.

A person is usually described as legendary after death, hence the even more exalted status of someone referred to as a 'living legend'. Legends are those individuals who leave the realm of history behind and enter the realm of lore. We no longer do historical research about them unless we are pedants or academics; what matters is the myths and stories told and written about them, rather than the actual evidence of their lives and deeds. This takes us directly to the Latin etymology of the term legend as 'a text to be read' rather than interrogated or critiqued.

Legendary individuals emerge in many walks of life. Sports; the arts; the military; business; and, very rarely, politics all spawn their legends. Legends leave a legacy that may include various artefacts, business or other empires, works of art, trophies, and so forth. Above all, however, they leave stories of a particular sort— stories that defy verification and, instead, invite, indeed demand, veneration. In telling the story of a legendary individual, narrator and audiences strike a special type of narrative contract, which allows or even encourages the narrator to engage in every kind of exaggeration, invention and fantasy, so long as it enhances the legendary status of the protagonist.

Particular events can also be legendary, even if none of their protagonists are legends—the 1980 Wimbledon final between Borg and McEnroe is sometimes referred to as legendary, even if neither of the competitors is generally regarded as a legend. People who watched it live or even on television may later boast that they were present when history was made, which means precisely the opposite. They experienced an event that escapes from the constraints of history and ensconces itself in the domain of story.

What then made Yevgeny Mravinsky legendary? To a relatively narrow circle of music lovers, the immediate answer would be the exceptional and never-to-be-repeated playing of the Leningrad Philharmonic, of which we have many recordings as testament. The fact that, as with Sviatoslav Richter, his performances were reverentially spoken of in the

West long before they could be experienced live or in recording adds to the mystique. So too does the fact that he, an aristocrat, somehow escaped every Stalinist purge—this in spite of premiering six of Shostakovich's symphonies, even when the latter lived in fear of his life. I suspect that Mravinsky's remarkable looks also contributed to the mystique, as did various anecdotes recounted about him.

Mravinsky is only known to a relatively small group of classical music enthusiasts today, most of whom will defend his legendary standing. His recordings in many regards remain unmatched. His interpretations of Tchaikovsky symphonies, for example, are not just the fastest and most furious imaginable but also evoke emotions, passions, and a terror that are entirely unattainable today. Compare the chainsaw screech of the 1950s Soviet brass and the pandemonium of its whistling woodwind to the round and uniform sound produced by today's symphony orchestras, and you realize that the Leningrad sound is gone forever.

It is not surprising then that a recording of Eighth Symphony by Shostakovich by Mravinsky and the Leningrad Philharmonic from the Royal Festival Hall takes pride of place in a twenty-CD BBC set called simply *BBC Legends: Great Recordings form the Archive.* This performance of one of Shostakovich's greatest symphonies, one which had been rarely heard in the West before, was recorded live at the Royal Festival Hall in September 1960 and leaves today's listener shattered. Many in the audience must have been perplexed by music they were hearing for the first time. The near constant coughing and shuffling and the primitive sound of the recording may make this a less than enjoyable listening experience. And yet, it is a recording that can rightly claim, at least for a circle of connoisseurs, to have preserved for posterity a legendary performance by a legendary conductor.

Now consider a different conductor, Herbert von Karajan, one who assiduously cultivated his personality cult on and off the podium with images of himself flying planes, skiing in Switzerland, and driving fast automobiles. He was probably even better-looking and far better recorded than Mravinsky, but the very narcissism that strove for legendary status seemed to work against him. Trying too hard to be a legend can undermine the effect.

Today, most music critics, at least in English-speaking countries, are rather sniffy about Karajan's legacy and, in my view, far too dismissive. I personally greatly enjoy many of his recordings that now routinely attract adjectives like 'glib', 'over-polished', plush, and outdated. However, there is one occasion that even his sternest critics acknowledge as legendary—the 1987 New Year Concert in Vienna, often seen as the greatest of them all. Even *The Gramophone* magazine, generally not his keenest advocate, used the 'L word' to describe this concert.

Are there many other classical musicians who may justify the label of legendary? Using *BBC Legends: Great Recordings form the Archive* as our starting point, it is easy to see that 'legends' usually include artists who belonged to a bygone era, such as Soviet artists like Rostropovich, Oistrakh, Kogan, and Gilels. Other legendary artists from the past, like Caruso, Heifetz, Rubinstein, Casals, Horowitz, and Callas, reached wider audiences and attracted mass followings, contributing to their popularity well outside the community of classical music lovers. Others who can claim the title of legendary are wayward geniuses like Arturo Benedetti Michelangeli and Glenn Gould, who created a mystique and a cult following. And then, as in every other field, there are those who became legendary, in part at least, because they died young, like horn player Dennis Brain and violinist Michael Rabin, who died in their thirties.

One could name several musicians who might have become legends had they died younger and left but a small number of treasured recordings rather than discographies stretching several metres of CDs. By becoming too familiar, they lost the mystique necessary to qualify as legendary. Still, Sviatoslav Richter, who lived a long life and of whom there are hundreds of authorized recordings and thousands of unauthorized ones, is safely ensconced in the legend pantheon.

Among living artists, I would suspect that many music lovers would defend Martha Argerich as legendary; her concerts are guaranteed to sell out, even when her repertoire has diminished in size, if not in excitement. Her every appearance is 'an event' and, appropriately enough for a legend, not liable to the type of critical scrutiny accorded to other artists. Instead, it is a quasi-religious experience enabling audiences to think, *One day I will be able to tell others that I attended an Argerich concert.*

So, where does this leave us with the word 'legendary'? It seems to me that someone becomes legendary when they become part of our unconscious mind as a larger-than-life phenomenon, a figure of myth and mystique that defies critical appraisals and objective judgements. In the world of music, a fluffed note (or indeed handfuls of them) or a memory lapse from a legend does not undermine the legend's standing but, if anything, augments it. A legend's wrong notes, to coin a phrase, are infinitely better than the talented musician's correct ones.

Legends are still in the making today, but they are unlikely to be the ones cultivated in celebrity hothouses or hyped up by the promoters, impresarios, and publicity agents who now dominate the classical music industry. There will always be musical legends because we, the music lovers, need them or even crave them. Just as sports fans need their sporting legends, music lovers need their musical legends. We need our legends to sustain our passions, to compare and judge others by them, and to hope that a few times in our lives we may have the privilege of seeing or hearing a legendary performer or attending an event that may become legendary. In this regard, having brushed past a legend or to have been part of a legendary event becomes part of our own life stories, a part of our identity that can be immensely valuable and life-enhancing.

Eventually, most old legends fade away as they are bound to do. New legends are needed to replace them. Who remembers now once legendary performers like pianist Josef Hofmann or violinist Josef Hassid? Well, a few of us do, but our fast-moving world calls for new legends. It will be interesting to know which of today's legends maintain their legendary standing in fifty or a hundred years' time. And who, among today's many outstanding young artists, will eventually become legends in their own right.

In Praise of Music

Having spent a large part of my life studying stories and storytelling, I firmly believe in stories with proper plots—with beginnings, middle, and ends. Not for me the open-ended stories with diffuse plots and indeterminate endings. I believe, therefore, that the reader who has followed me along this musical journey is entitled to a proper conclusion, an endpoint of the journey and maybe the starting point of a different journey.

What better way to end this journey than by celebrating music, without which our lives, at least the lives of us music lovers, would be so poor, empty and meaningless? 'Music gives a soul to the universe, wings to the mind, flight to the imagination and life to everything.' Does it matter that Plato probably never wrote or uttered these words? The sentiment is true, at least most of the time.

Music directly touches our emotions even without recourse to words or images, in ways that no other art does. It consoles us when we are low, rouses us when we are depleted, stimulates us when we are excited, entertains us when we are bored, and inspires us whatever our mood may be. When dragged down by the follies and pettiness of daily life, music can lift us above the mundane and the parochial. There are times when it stirs the very core of our being and forces us to question our deepest convictions and to face our deepest vulnerabilities.

For me and classical music enthusiasts like me, Bach, Mozart, Beethoven, Schubert, and the other great composers whose music fills our daily lives, these are not just historical figures; they are members of our daily life with whom we commune routinely. They are also figures towards whom I feel a great deal of gratitude and love.

Without Bach, to whom would I turn for reassurance that the great river of life will continue to flow past our current troubles and adversities?

Without Mozart, to whom would I turn for light in times of darkness?

Without Beethoven, who would I turn to for inspiration when obstacles block my path?

Without Schubert, to whom would I turn for a belief that there is something sublime in the universe?

Without Rossini and Johann Strauss, to whom would I turn to for effervescence and cheer?

Without Mahler, to whom would I turn to for provocation and intellectual challenge?

Without Shostakovich, who would accompany me in my visits to the darkest darkness?

In 1817, the twenty-year-old Franz Schubert composed his hymn to music, a three-minute masterpiece that moves everyone who hears it. The music itself transforms a pleasant little poem that would have long been forgotten into something eternal and sublime, something that expresses perfectly my own feelings as I reach the end of this musical journey.

As I cannot reproduce Schubert's musical miracle, I can at least close with the text that inspired it and urge my reader to look for any recording of the song.

O blessed art, how often in dark hours,
When the savage ring of life tightens
round me,

Have you kindled warm love in my heart,
Have transported me to a better world!
Transported to a better world

Often a sigh has escaped from your harp,
A sweet, sacred harmony of yours

Has opened up the heavens to better times
for me,
O blessed art, I thank you for that!
O blessed art, I thank you!

(Franz Schubert, 'An die Musik,' D547;
Poem by Franz Von Schober, translation
from Wikipedia)

Index

Endorsements

Imagine a friend who loved music, and who would keep saying interesting things about the music they loved. Their taste is not the same as yours, but their comments and stories make you want to listen to some of their favourite music, and also give you a different appreciation of the music that you love. Then imagine that this friend's interesting comments were grounded in hours and years of intense listening, that they had an unusual perspective to bring to the party (music as story), and that they said it all with grace and eloquence, and with the light touch of a gossip column. That is what this book is like. Enjoy it, and have your streaming device ready to explore!

David Sims, Storyteller, Musician, Emeritus Professor of Organizational Behaviour City University,

In a world where commerce dictates the Arts, it is a joy to read this book, written with love and deep understanding as a heartfelt response to real music by my friend Yiannis, a fellow traveller in search of musical truth!

Bruno Schrecker (cellist with the Allegri String Quartet 1968-1999)

'This a book for music lovers' says Yiannis Gabriel. The notion of love is crucial here. Academic musicology, however useful and insightful, rarely if ever, touches on the subjective experience of listening to music. But to believe that music is an objective experience, which can be adequately explained in scientific (or quasi-scientific) terms, or reduced to a socio-political epiphenomenon, is an illusion - comforting to some perhaps, but deadly when it comes to the individual's experience of discovering and learning to love a musical work. As with all things that matter to us, we try to make sense of music, not through factual analysis, but by weaving stories in our imaginations. This is both an intensely creative and an intensely personal experience. As the philosopher Ernst Bloch put it, 'When we listen to music, what we really hear is ourselves.' Yiannis Gabriel's book is a highly personal account of his experience or music: of the stories it has told to him and of the life-experiences in which those stories have played a very positive part. Far from being solipsistic or self-indulgent, far from telling us what we *should* hear when we listen to music, it invites us to follow his example and find stories and meanings of our own within the musical works he loves best. These are those for whom, in Nietzsche's famous phrase, 'Without music, life would be a mistake'. On reading this book, the conclusion we reach is that, with music's help, life is not a mistake, but a creative adventure.

Stephen Johnson, composer, author, musicologist

This is a wonderful book about music. Yiannis Gabriel's depth of knowledge and the infectious enthusiasm he has for the music he loves radiates through every chapter. He makes you think about your own responses to music you already know, and he is also a willing guide to music that may be less familiar. He has listened carefully to more music than most of us, both joyfully and seriously. Read the book, listen to the music, go for a walk. You will feel better for it.

Nigel Beaham-Powell, Composer and Subject Leader in Commercial Music, Bath Spa University

From the golden age of western classical listening, Gabriel's eloquent voice reminds us how moving classical music can be.

Daniel Leech-Wilkinson, Emeritus Professor of Music, King's College London

Music and Story

Yiannis Gabriel is a Greek psychologist who has spent a large part of his life studying and writing about myths and stories. After a degree in mechanical engineering, he studied social psychology in London and Berkeley obtaining a PhD with a dissertation on Sigmund Freud. He subsequently worked for forty years in British higher education institutions, including Imperial College, Royal Holloway and the University of Bath. During this period, he published ten books and numerous articles, edited several journals and ran a storytelling seminar.

As a Greek, Yiannis has always been fascinated by myths and stories, using his psychoanalytic knowledge to study narratives as opening windows into many political, cultural and organizational phenomena. Stories may not provide reliable accounts of actual events, but they reveal our deeper desires and fears. The truth of a story lies not in its accuracy but in its deeper meaning. Accordingly, Yiannis has explored storytelling as a way of studying a wide range of topics including leader-follower relations, nostalgia, insults, apologies, job loss, conspiracy theories and institutional failures. Many of his works explore the relevance of ancient Greek myths for today's world. This book draws together his fascination with stories with his lifelong love of classical music.

He maintains an active blog at yiannisgabriel.com